P. (Patrick) Brydone

A Tour through Sicily and Malta

In a Series of Letters to William Beckford, esq. of Somerly in Suffolk: Vol. II.

P. (Patrick) Brydone

A Tour through Sicily and Malta
In a Series of Letters to William Beckford, esq. of Somerly in Suffolk: Vol. II.

ISBN/EAN: 9783337211325

Printed in Europe, USA, Canada, Australia, Japan

Cover: Foto ©Andreas Hilbeck / pixelio.de

More available books at **www.hansebooks.com**

A TOUR

THROUGH

SICILY AND MALTA.

IN A

SERIES OF LETTERS

TO

WILLIAM BECKFORD, Esq.

OF SOMERLY IN SUFFOLK;

FROM

P. BRYDONE. F. R. S.

A NEW EDITION.

VOL. II.

LONDON:

PRINTED FOR W. STRAHAN; AND
T. CADELL, IN THE STRAND.
M DCC LXXVI.

CONTENTS

OF THE

SECOND VOLUME.

LETTER XVII. p. 1.

SAIL for Agrigentum.—Ifland of Gozzo.—Coaſt of Sicily.—American aloes.—City of Agrigentum.

LETTER XVIII. p. 10.

Antiquities of Agrigentum.—Temples of Venus—Of Concord—Of Hercules—Of Jupiter Olympus, &c.—Celebrated picture of Zeuxis—Statue of Apollo.—Catacombs and ſepulchres.—Mountain of Agrigentum.

CONTENTS.

LETTER XIX. p. 20.

Luxury of the ancient Agrigentini.—Hospitality.—Anecdote.—Humanity and gratitude to their horses.—Agrigentum long subject to tyrants.—Phalaris, anecdote of him.—Melanippus and Cariton, their friendship.—Death of Phalaris.

LETTER XX. p. 36.

Country around Agrigentum.—A feast.—Hospitality of the Agrigentini.—Their character.—The bishop.—Departure for Trapani.—Sea storm.—Driven back to Agrigentum.—Journey by land to Palermo.—Richness and beauty of the country.—Poverty and oppression of the peasants.

LETTER XXI. p. 59.

Conclusion of the journey to Palermo.—Contrast betwixt Sicily and Switzerland—Inns, &c.

CONTENTS.

LETTER XXII. p. 73.

City of Palermo—Marino.—Converſations where held.—Sicilian ladies.—Reflections.

LETTER XXIII. p. 84.

The viceroy—His table—Nobility.—Their temperance—Gallantry.—Young ladies—Their education.

LETTER XXIV. p. 93.

Bagaria—Palace of the Prince Patagonia.

LETTER XXV. p. 104.

Sirocc wind.—Convent of capuchins—Their burial place. Method of preſerving the dead.—Anecdote.—Addreſs of a Sicilian ſervant.

LETTER XXVI. p. 140.

Account of a comet.—Reflections.

CONTENTS.

LETTER XXVII. p. 168.

Cathedral of Palermo.—Jesuits church.—Cathedral of Monreale.—The archbishop.—Preparations for a festival.—Superstition of the people.

LETTER XXVIII. p. 180.

St. Rosolia.—Subject of an Epic poem.—Some account of her.—St. Viar.—Reflections.

LETTER XXIX. p. 190.

Sirocc wind.—Review of a Swiss regiment.—Entertainment.—Difference of education here and on the continent.—Prince of Resuttana.

LETTER XXX. p. 209.

Feast of St. Rosolia.

CONTENTS.

LETTER XXXI. p. 241.

Antiquities.—Camesena.—Temple of Ceres at Enna.—Temple of Venus Erecina.—Difference of Homer and Virgil in their accounts of Sicily.

LETTER XXXII. p. 256.

Monte Pelegrino.—St. Rosolia.—Ancient fortress.—Situation of Palermo.—Antiquity of that city.—Inscriptions.

LETTER XXXIII. p. 272.

Utility of ices in a hot climate.—Sicilian fisheries.—The Tunny fish.—The Pesce Spada, or Sword fish.—Method of fishing in the night.—Coral fishing.—Oppression of the government.—Foundation of the feudal system in Sicily.—Parliament.—Inquisition.—Power of the viceroy.—Military force.—Bandiere men.

CONTENTS.

LETTER XXXIV. p. 297.

Sicilian titles.—Luxury of the Sicilians in their carriages.—Ridiculous prejudice.

LETTER XXXV. p. 306.

Sicilians animated in converſation.—Marriage ceremonies.—Beauty of the ladies.—Anecdote.—Poetry the univerſal paſſion of the Sicilians.

LETTER XXXVI. p. 318.

The opera.—Gabrieli, her wonderful performance—Her caprice.—Ballet of the opera.—Engliſh characters taken off.—Enmity betwixt the Sicilians and Neapolitans.

LETTER XXXVII. p. 337.

Remarkable ſprings in Sicily.—Sulphureous baths.—Springs of warm water in the ſea.—Gigantic bones.—Crops of wheat.—Method

CONTENTS.

Method of preserving their grain.—Commodities of Sicily.—Soda.—Wild honey.—Sugar.—Liquorice.—Oranges.—Pistachio nuts.—Manna.—Cantharides.—Marbles.—Pietra Saponaro.—Mushroom stone, &c.—Mount Ætna—Advantages resulting from it.

LETTER XXXVIII. p. 352.
Return to Naples.

A TOUR

THROUGH

SICILY AND MALTA.

LETTER XVII.

DEAR BECKFORD, *Agrigentum, June 11th.*

WE left the port of Malta in a fparonaro which we hired to convey us to this city.

We coafted along the ifland, and went to take a view of the north-port, its fortifications and lazaretto. All thefe are very great, and more like the works of a mighty and powerful people, than of fo fmall a ftate.

ſtate. The mortars cut out of the rock are a tremendous invention. There are about fifty of them, near the different creeks and landing-places round the iſland. They are directed at the moſt probable ſpots where boats would attempt a landing. The mouths of ſome of theſe mortars are about ſix feet wide, and they are ſaid to throw a hundred cantars of cannon-ball or ſtones. A cantar is, I think, about a hundred pound weight; ſo that if they do take place, they muſt make a dreadful havock amongſt a debarkation of boats.

The diſtance of Malta from Gozzo is not above four or five miles, and the ſmall iſland of Commino lies betwixt them. The coaſts of all the three are bare and barren, but covered over with towers, redoubts, and fortifications of various kinds.

As Gozzo is ſuppoſed to be the celebrated iſland of Calypſo, you may believe we expected

pected something very fine; but we were disappointed. It must either be greatly fallen off since the time she inhabited it, or the archbishop of Cambray, as well as Homer, must have flattered greatly in their painting. We looked, as we went along the coast, for the grotto of the goddess, but could see nothing that resembled it. Neither could we observe those verdant banks eternally covered with flowers; nor those lofty trees for ever in blossom, that lost their heads in the clouds, and afforded a shade to the sacred baths of her and her nymphs. We saw, indeed, some nymphs; but as neither Calypso nor Eucharis seemed to be of the number, we paid little attention to them, and I was in no apprehension about my Telemachus: Indeed, it would have required an imagination as strong as Don Quixote's, to have brought about the metamorphosis.

Finding our hopes frustrated, we ordered our sailors to pull out to sea, and bid adieu to the island of Calypso, concluding, either that our intelligence was false, or that both the island and its inhabitants were greatly changed. We soon found ourselves once more at the mercy of the waves: Night came on, and our rowers began their evening song to the Virgin, and beat time with their oars. Their offering was acceptable; for we had the most delightful weather. We wrapt ourselves up in our cloaks, and slept most comfortably, having provided mattrasses at Malta. By a little after day-break, we found we had got without sight of all the islands, and saw only a part of mount Ætna smoking above the waters. The wind sprung up fair, and by ten o'clock we had sight of the coast of Sicily.

On considering the smallness of our boat, and the great breadth of this passage, we could not help admiring the temerity of these people, who, at all seasons of the year, venture to Sicily in these diminutive vessels;

vessels; yet it is very seldom that any accident happens; they are so perfectly acquainted with the weather, foretelling, almost to a certainty, every storm, many hours before it comes on. The sailors look upon this passage as one of the most stormy and dangerous in the Mediterranean. It is called the canal of Malta, and is much dreaded by the Levant ships; but indeed, at this season, there is no danger.

We arrived at Sicily a little before sunset, and landed opposite to Ragusa, and not far from the ruins of the little Hybla; the third town of that name in the island, distinguished by the epithets of the Great (near mount Ætna), the Lesser (near Augusta), and the Little (just by Ragusa). Here we found a fine sandy beach, and whilst the servants were employed in dressing supper, we amused ourselves with bathing and gathering shells, of which there is a considerable variety. We were in expectation of finding the nautilus, for which this island is famous; but in this we did not succeed. However, we picked up some handsome shells, though not equal to those that are brought from the Indies.

After supper, we again launched our bark, and went to sea. The wind was favourable as we could wish. We had our nightly serenade as usual, and the next day, by twelve o'clock, we reached the celebrated port of Agrigentum.

The captain of the port gave us a polite reception, and insisted on accompanying us to the city, which stands near the top of a mountain, four miles distant from the harbour, and about eleven hundred feet above the level of the sea. The road on each side is bordered by a row of exceeding large American aloes: upwards of one third of them being at present in full blow, and making the most beautiful appearance

pearance that can be imagined. The flower-ſtems of this noble plant are in general betwixt twenty and thirty feet high, (ſome of them more) and are covered with flowers from top to bottom; which taper regularly, and form a beautiful kind of pyramid, the baſe or pedeſtal of which is the fine ſpreading leaves of the plant. As this is eſteemed, in northern countries, one of the greateſt curioſities of the vegetable tribe, we were happy at ſeeing it in ſo great perfection; much greater, I think, than I had ever ſeen it before.

With us, I think, it is vulgarly reckoned, (though I believe falſely) that they only flower once in a hundred years. Here I was informed, that, at the lateſt, they always blow the ſixth year; but for the moſt part the fifth.—As the whole ſubſtance of the plant is carried into the ſtem and the flowers, the leaves begin to decay as ſoon as the blow is completed, and a numerous offspring of young plants are produced round the root of the old one; thefe are flip'd off, and formed into new plantations, either for hedges or for avenues to their country-houfes.

The city of Agrigentum, now called *Girgenti*, is irregular and ugly; though from a few miles diftance at fea, it makes a noble appearance, little inferior to that of Genoa.—As it lies on the flope of the mountain, the houfes do not hide one another; but every part of the city is feen.

On our arrival, we found a great falling off indeed; the houfes are mean, the ftreets dirty, crooked, and narrow.—It ftill contains near twenty thoufand people; a fad reduction from its ancient grandeur, when it was faid to confift of no lefs than eight hundred thoufand, being the next city to Syracufe for numbers.

The

The Canonico Spoto, from Mr. Hamilton's letter, and from our former acquaintance with him at Naples, gave us a kind and a hofpitable reception. He infifted on our being his guefts; and we are now in his houfe, comfortably lodged, and elegantly entertained, which, after our crowded little apartment in the fparonaro, is by no means a difagreeable change.—Farewell. I fhall write you again foon.

Ever yours.

LETTER XVIII.

Agrigentum, June 12th.

WE are juft now returned from examining the antiquities of Agrigentum, the moft confiderable, perhaps, of any in Sicily.

The ruins of the ancient city lie about a fhort mile from the modern one. Thefe, like the ruins of Syracufe, are moftly converted into corn-fields, vineyards, and orchards; but the remains of the temples here, are much more confpicuous than thofe of Syracufe. Four of thefe have ftood pretty much in a right line, near the fouth wall of the city. The firft they call the temple of Venus; almoft one half of which ftill remains. The fecond is that of Concord: It may be confidered as entire, not one column having as yet fallen. It is precifely precisely of the same dimensions and same architecture as that of Venus, which had probably served as the model for it. By the following inscription, found on a large piece of marble, it appears to have been built at the expence of the Lilibitani; probably after having been defeated by the people of Agrigentum.

CONCORDIÆ AGRIGENTINORUM SACRUM,
RESPUBLICA LILIBITANORUM,
DEDICANTIBUS M. ATTERIO CANDIDO
PROCOS. ET L. CORNELIO MAR-
CELLO. Q. P. R. P. R.

These temples are supported by thirteen large fluted Doric columns on each side; and six at each end. All their bases, capitals, entablatures, &c. still remain entire; and as the architecture is perfectly simple, without any thing affected or studied, the whole strikes the eye at once, and pleases very much. The columns are, indeed, shorter than the common Doric proportions;

and

and they certainly are not so elegant as some of the ancient temples near Rome, and in other places in Italy.

The third temple is that of Hercules, altogether in ruins; but appears to have been of a much greater size than the former two. We measured some of the broken columns, near seven feet in diameter. It was here that the famous statue of Hercules stood, so much celebrated by Cicero; which the people of Agrigentum defended with such bravery, against Verres, who attempted to seize it. You will find the whole story in his pleadings against that infamous prætor.

There was likewise in this temple a famous picture by Zeuxis. Hercules was represented in his cradle killing the two serpents: Alcmena and Amphitrion having just entered the apartment, were painted with every mark of terror and astonishment

ment. Pliny fays, the painter looked upon this piece as invaluable; and therefore could never be prevailed on to put a price upon it, but gave it as a prefent to Agrigentum, to be placed in the temple of Hercules. Thefe two great mafter-pieces have been loft. We thought of them with regret, whilft we trod on thefe venerable ruins.

Near to this lie ruins of the temple of Jupiter Olympus, fuppofed by the Sicilian authors to have been the largeft in the heathen world. It is now called *il tempio de' giganti*, or the Giants Temple, as the people cannot conceive that fuch maffes of rock could ever be put together by the hands of ordinary men. The fragments of columns are indeed enormous, and give us a vaft idea of this fabric. It is faid to have ftood till the year 1100; but is now a perfect ruin. Our Cicerones affured us, it was exactly the fame dimenfions with the church of St. Peter at Rome: But in this they are egregiously mistaken.—St. Peter's being much greater than any thing that ever the heathen world produced.

There are the remains of many more temples, and other great works; but these, I think, are the most conspicuous. They shew you that of Vulcan, of Proserpine, of Castor and Pollux, and a very remarkable one of Juno. This too was enriched by one of the most famous pictures of antiquity; which is celebrated by many of the ancient writers.—Zeuxis was determined to excel every thing that had gone before him, and to form a model of human perfection. To this end, he prevailed on all the finest women of Agrigentum, who were even ambitious of the honour, to appear naked before him. Of these he chose five for his models, and moulding all the perfections of these beauties into one, he composed the picture of the goddess. This was ever looked upon

SICILY AND MALTA.

on as his mafter-piece; but was unfortunately burnt when the Carthaginians took Agrigentum.—Many of the citizens retired into this temple as to a place of fafety; but as foon as they found the gates attacked by the enemy, they agreed to fet fire to it, and chofe rather to perifh in the flames, than fubmit to the power of the conquerors. However, neither the deftruction of the temple, nor the lofs of their lives, has been fo much regretted by pofterity, as the lofs of this picture.

The temple of Æfculapius (the ruins of which are ftill to be feen) was not lefs celebrated for a ftatue of Apollo. It was taken from them by the Carthaginians, at the fame time that the temple of Juno was burnt. It was carried off by the conquerors, and continued the greateft ornament of Carthage for many years, and was at laft reftored by Scipio, at the final deftruction of that city. Some of the Sicilians allege,

allege, I believe without any ground, that it was afterwards carried to Rome, and ſtill remains there, the wonder of all ages; known to the whole world under the name of the Apollo of Belvidere; and allowed to be the perfection of human art.

I ſhould be very tedious, were I to give you a minute deſcription of every piece of antiquity. Indeed, little or nothing is to be learned from the greateſt part of them. The ancient walls of the city are moſtly cut out of the rock; the catacombs and ſepulchres are all very great: One of theſe is worthy particular notice, becauſe it is mentioned by Polybius, as being oppoſite to the temple of Hercules, and to have been ſtruck by lightning even in his time. It remains almoſt entire, and anſwers the deſcription he gives of it: The inſcriptions are ſo defaced, that we could make nothing of them.

This

This is the monument of Tero king of Agrigentum, one of the firſt of the Sicilian tyrants. The great antiquity of it may be gathered from this, that Tero is not only mentioned by Diodorus, Polybius, and the later of the ancient hiſtorians; but likewiſe by Herodotus, and Pindar, who dedicates two of his Olympic odes to him: So that this monument muſt be more than two thouſand years old. It is a kind of pyramid, probably one of the moſt durable forms.

All theſe mighty ruins of Agrigentum, and the whole mountain on which it ſtands, are compoſed of a concretion of ſeaſhells, run together, and cemented by a kind of ſand or gravel, and now become as hard, and perhaps more durable than even marble itſelf. This ſtone is white before it has been expoſed to the air; but in the temples and other ruins, it is become of a dark brown. I ſhall bring home ſome pieces

pieces of it for the infpection of the curious. I found thefe fhells on the very fummit of the mountain, at leaft fourteen or fifteen hundred feet above the level of the fea. They are of the commoneft kinds, cockles, muffels, oyfters, &c.

" The things we know are neither rich nor rare;
" But wonder how the devil they got there."
POPE.

By what means they have been lifted up to this vaft height, and fo intimately mixed with the fubftance of the rock, I leave to you and your philofophical friends to determine.—This old battered globe of ours, has probably fuffered many convulfions not recorded in any hiftory.—You have heard of the vaft Stratum of bones lately difcovered in Iftria and Offero;—part of it runs below rocks of marble, upwards of forty feet in thicknefs, and they have not yet been able to afcertain its extent: Something of the fame kind has been found in Dalmatia,
in

in the iflands of the Archipelago; and lately, I am told, in the rock of Gibraltar.— Now, the deluge recorded in Scripture, will hardly account for all the appearances of this fort to be met with, almoft in every country in the world.—But I am interrupted by vifitors;—which is a lucky circumftance, both for you and me; for I was juft going to be very philofophical, and confequently very dull. Adieu.

LETTER XIX.

Agrigentum, June 13th.

THE interruption in my laſt, was a deputation from the biſhop, to invite us to a great dinner to-morrow at the port; ſo that we ſhall know whether this place ſtill deſerves the character of luxury, it always held amongſt the ancients: We have great reaſon to think, from the politeneſs and attention we have met with, that it has never loſt its ancient hoſpitality, for which it was likewiſe ſo much celebrated.

Plato, when he viſited Sicily, was ſo much ſtruck with the luxury of Agrigentum, both in their houſes and their tables, that a ſaying of his is ſtill recorded: That they built as if they were never to die, and eat as if they had not an hour to live.

It

It is preserved by Ælian, and is just now before me.

He tells a story by way of illustration, which shews a much greater conformity of manners, than one could have expected, betwixt the young nobility amongst the ancients, and our own at this day.

He says, that after a great feast, where there was a number of young people of the first fashion, they got all so much intoxicated, that from their reeling and tumbling upon one another, they imagined they were at sea, in a storm, and began to think themselves in the most imminent danger: at last they agreed, that the only way to save their lives was to lighten the ship, and with one accord began to throw the rich furniture out of the windows, to the great edification of the mob below; and did not stop till they had entirely cleared the house of it, which, from this exploit, was ever after denominated the *triremes*, or the ship. He says it was one of the principal palaces of the city, and retained this name for ever after. In Dublin, I have been told, there are more than one triremes; and that this frolic, which they call throwing the house out of the window, is by no means uncommon.

At the same time that Agrigentum is abused by the ancient authors for its drunkenness, it is as much celebrated for its hospitality; and I believe, it will be found, that this virtue, and this vice, have ever had a sort of sneaking kindness for each other, and have generally gone hand in hand, both in ancient and in modern times. The Swiss, the Scots, and the Irish, who are at present the most drunken people in Europe, are likewise, in all probability, the most hospitable; whereas in the very sober countries, Spain, Portugal, and Italy, hospitality is a virtue very little known, or indeed

indeed any other virtue, except fobriety; which has been produced, probably a good deal from the tyranny of their government, and their dread of the inquifition; for where every perfon is in fear, left his real fentiments fhould appear, it would be very dangerous to unlock his heart; but in countries where there are neither civil nor ecclefiaftical tyrants to lay an embargo on our thoughts, people are under no apprehenfion left they fhould be known.

However, thefe are not the only reafons. The moral virtues and vices may fometimes depend on natural caufes.—The very elevated fituation of this city, where the air is exceedingly thin and cold, has perhaps been one reafon why its inhabitants are fonder of wine than their neighbours in the valleys.

The fame may be faid of the three nations I have mentioned; the greateft part

part of their countries lying amongſt hills and mountains, where the climate renders ſtrong liquors more neceſſary; or, at leaſt, leſs pernicious, than in low places.—It is not ſurpriſing, that this practice, probably begun amongſt the mountains, where the air is ſo keen, has by degrees crept down into the valleys, and has at laſt become almoſt epidemical in thoſe countries.

Fazzello, after railing at Agrigentum for its drunkenneſs, adds, that there was no town in the iſland ſo celebrated for its hoſpitality. He ſays that many of the nobles had ſervants placed at the gates of the city, to invite all ſtrangers to their houſes. It is in reference to this probably, that Empedocles ſays, that even the gates of the city proclaimed a welcome to every ſtranger. From our experience we are well entitled to ſay, that the people of Agrigentum ſtill retain this antiquated virtue, ſo little known in polite countries. To-morrow we ſhall

have

have a better opportunity of judging whether it is ſtill accompanied by its ſiſter vice.

The accounts that the old authors give of the magnificence of Agrigentum are amazing; though indeed there are none of them that proclaim it in ſtronger terms than the monuments that ſtill remain.—Diodorus ſays, the great veſſels for holding water were commonly of ſilver, and the litters and carriages for the moſt part were of ivory richly adorned. He mentions a pond made at an immenſe expence, full of fiſh and of water-fowl, that in his time was the great reſort of the inhabitants, on their feſtivals; but he ſays, that even then (in the age of Auguſtus) it was going to ruin, requiring too great an expence to keep it up. There is not now the ſmalleſt veſtige of it: But there is ſtill to be ſeen a curious ſpring of water that throws up a kind of oil on its ſurface, which

which is made use of by the poor people in many diseases. This is supposed to mark out the place of the celebrated pond; which is recorded by Pliny and Solinus to have abounded with this oil.

Diodorus, speaking of the riches of Agrigentum, mentions one of its citizens returning victorious from the Olympic games, and entering his city, attended by three hundred chariots, each drawn by four white horses, richly caparisoned; and gives many other instances of their vast profusion and luxury.

Those horses, according to that author, were esteemed all over Greece, for their beauty and swiftness; and their race is celebrated by many of the ancient writers.

" Arduus inde Agragas ostentat maxima longe
" Moenia, magnanimum quondam generator
    " equorum,"

says

says Virgil in the third Æneid; and Pliny acquaints us, that those which had been often victorious at the games were not only honoured with burial rites, but had magnificent monuments erected to eternize their memory. This Timeus confirms: He tells us, that he saw at Agrigentum several pyramids built as sepulchral monuments to celebrated horses; he adds that when those animals became old and unfit for service, they were always taken care of, and spent the remainder of their lives in ease and plenty.—I could wish that our countrymen would imitate the gratitude and humanity of the Sicilians in this article; at least, the latter part of it. I don't know that our nation can so justly be taxed with cruelty or ingratitude in any other article as in their treatment of horses, the animal that of all others is the most entitled to our care. How piteous a thing it is, on many of your great roads, to see the finest old hunters, that were once the

glory

glory of the chace, condemned, in the decline of life, to the tyranny of the moſt cruel oppreſſors; in whoſe hands they ſuffer the moſt extreme miſery, till they at laſt ſink under the taſk that is aſſigned them. I am called away to ſee ſome more antiques, but ſhall finiſh this letter to-night, as the poſt goes off for Italy to-morrow morning,

13th; Afternoon. We have ſeen a great many old walls and vaults that little or nothing can be made of. They give them names, and pretend to tell you what they were, but as they bear no reſemblance to thoſe things now, it would be no leſs idle to trouble you with their nonſenſe than to believe it. We have indeed ſeen one thing that has amply repaid us for the trouble we have taken. It is the repreſentation of a boar-hunting, in alto relievo, on white marble; and is at leaſt equal, if not ſuperior, to any thing of the kind I have met with

SICILY AND MALTA. 29

with in Italy. It confifts of four different parts, which form the hiftory of this remarkable chace and its confequences.

The firft is the preparation for the hunt. There are twelve hunters, with each his lance, and a fhort hanger under his left arm of a very fingular form. The dogs refemble thofe we call lurchers. The horfes are done with great fire and fpirit, and are perhaps a better proof of the excellence of the race, than even the teftimony of their authors; for the artift that formed thefe muft certainly have been accuftomed to fee very fine horfes.

The fecond piece reprefents the chace.— The third the death of the king, by a fall from his horfe.—And the fourth, the defpair of the queen and her attendants receiving the news. She is reprefented falling down in a fwoon, and fupported by her women, who are all of admirable workmanfhip;

It is executed in the moſt maſterly ſtyle, and is indeed one of the fineſt remains of antiquity. It is preſerved in the great church, which is noted through all Sicily for a remarkable echo; ſomething in the manner of our whiſpering gallery at St. Paul's, though more difficult to be accounted for.

If one perſon ſtands at the weſt-gate, and another places himſelf on the cornice, at the moſt diſtant point of the church, exactly behind the great altar, they can hold a converſation in very low whiſpers.

For many years this ſingularity was little known; and ſeveral of the confeſſing chairs being placed near the great altar, the wags, who were in the secret, uſed to take their ſtation at the door of the cathedral; and by a boar-hounds heard diſtinctly every word betwixt the confeſſor and his penitent. You may believe, they did

SICILY AND MALTA.

did not fail to make their own use when occasion offered.—The most secret intrigues were discovered; and every woman in Agrigentum changed either her gallant or her confessor. Yet still it was the same.—At last, however, the cause was found out; the chairs were removed, and other precautions were taken, to prevent the discovery of these sacred mysteries; and a mutual amnesty passed amongst all the offended parties.

Agrigentum, like Syracuse, was long subject to the yoke of tyrants. Fazzello gives some account of their cruelty, but I have no intention of repeating it: One story, however, pleased me; it is a well known one, but as it is short, you shall have it.

Perillo, a goldsmith, by way of paying court to Phalaris the tyrant, made him a present of a brazen bull, of admirable workmanship;

manship; hollow within, and so contrived that the voice of a person shut up in it, sounded exactly like the bellowing of a real bull. The artist pointed out to the tyrant what an admirable effect this must produce, were he only to shut up a few criminals in it, and make a fire under them.

Phalaris, struck with so horrid an idea, and perhaps curious to try the experiment, told the goldsmith that he himself was the only person worthy of animating his bull: that he must have studied the note that made it roar to the greatest advantage, and that it would be unjust to deprive him of any part of the honour of his invention. Upon which he ordered the goldsmith to be shut up, and made a great fire around the bull; which immediately began to roar, to the admiration and delight of all Agrigentum. Cicero says, this bull was carried to Carthage at the taking of Agrigentum; and
was

SICILY AND MALTA.

was restored again by Scipio, after the destruction of that city.

Fazzello adds another story, which is still more to the honour of Phalaris. Two friends, Melanippus and Cariton, had conspired his death. Cariton, in hopes of saving his friend from the danger of the enterprise, determined to execute it alone. However, in his attempt to poignard the tyrant, he was seized by the guards, and immediately put to the torture, to make him confess his accomplice: this he bore with the utmost fortitude, refusing to make the discovery; 'till Melanippus, informed of the situation of his friend, ran to the tyrant, assuring him that he alone was the guilty person; that it was entirely by his instigation that Cariton had acted; and begged that he might be put on the rack in the place of his friend. Phalaris, struck with such heroism, pardoned them both.

Notwithstanding this generous action, he was in many respects a barbarous tyrant. Fazzello gives the following account of his death, with which I shall conclude this letter, for I am monstrously tired, and, I dare say, so are you. Zeno, the philosopher, came to Agrigentum, and being admitted into the presence of the tyrant, advised him, for his own comfort, as well as that of his subjects, to resign his power, and to lead a private life. Phalaris did not relish these philosophical sentiments; and suspecting Zeno to be in a conspiracy with some of his subjects, ordered him to be put to the torture in presence of the citizens of Agrigentum.

Zeno immediately began to reproach them with cowardice and pusillanimity in submitting tamely to the yoke of so worthless a tyrant; and in a short time raised such a flame, that they defeated the guards, and stoned Phalaris to death.—I dare say you are

are glad they did it so quickly.—Well, I shall not write such long letters for the future; for I assure you it is at least as troublesome to the writer as the reader. Adieu. We shall sail to-morrow or next morning for Trapani, from whence you may expect to hear from me. We are now going out to examine more antique walls, but I shall not trouble you with them.

Farewell.

LETTER XX.

June 16th.

WHEN I have nothing elſe to do, I generally take up the pen. We are now on the top of a high mountain, about half way betwixt Agrigentum and Palermo. Our ſea expedition by Trapani has failed, and we are determined to put no more confidence in that element, happy beyond meaſure to find ourſelves at a diſtance from it, though in the moſt wretched of villages. We have travelled all night on mules; and arrived here about ten o'clock, overcome with ſleep and fatigue. We have juſt had an excellent diſh of tea, which never fails to cure me of both; and I am now as freſh as when we ſet out. It has not had the ſame effect on my companions: they have thrown themſelves down on a vile ſtraw-bed

bed in the corner of the hovel; and in spite of a parcel of starved chickens, that are fluttering about and picking the straws all round them, they are already fast asleep.

I shall seize that time to recapitulate what has happened since my last.

The day after I wrote you, we made some little excursions round Agrigentum. The country is delightful; producing corn, wine, and oil, in the greatest abundance: the fields are, at the same time, covered with a variety of the finest fruits; oranges, lemons, pomegranates, almonds, pistachio-nuts, &c. These afforded us almost as agreeable an entertainment as the consideration of the ruins from whence they spring.

We dined with the bishop, according to agreement, and rose from table, convinced that the ancient Agrigentini could not pos-

D 3 sibly

sibly understand the true luxury of eating better than their descendants, to whom they have transmitted a very competent portion both of their social virtues and vices. I beg their pardon for calling them vices, I wish I had a softer name for it; it looks like ingratitude for their hospitality, for which we owe them so much.

We were just thirty at table, but, upon my word, I do not think we had less than an hundred dishes of meat. These were dressed with the richest and most delicate sauces; and convinced us that the old Roman proverb of "Siculus coquus et Sicula mensa," was not more applicable in their time, than it is at present. Nothing was wanting that could be invented to stimulate and to flatter the palate; and to create a false appetite as well as to satisfy it. Some of the very dishes so much relished by the Roman epicures made a part of the feast; particularly the morene, which is so often mentioned by their authors: it is a species of eel, found only in this part of the Mediterranean, and sent from hence to several of the courts of Europe. It is not so fat and luscious as other eels, so that you can eat a good deal more of it: its flesh is as white as snow, and is indeed a very great delicacy. But a modern refinement in luxury has, I think, still produced a greater: By a particular kind of management they make the livers of their fowls grow to a large size, and at the same time acquire a high and rich flavour. It is indeed a most incomparable dish; but the means of procuring it is so cruel, that I will not even trust it with you. Perhaps, without any bad intention, you might mention it to some of your friends, they to others, till at last it might come into the hands of those that would be glad to try the experiment; and the whole race of poultry might ever have reason to curse me: let it suffice to say, that it occasions a painful and lingering death to the poor animal ; that I know is enough to make you wish never to taste of it, whatever effect it may have upon others.

The Sicilians eat of every thing, and attempted to make us do the same. The company was remarkably merry, and did by no means belie their ancient character, for most of them were more than half seas over, long before we rose from table ; and I was somewhat apprehensive of a second edition of the Triremes scene, as they were beginning to reel exceedingly. By the bye, I do not doubt but that phrase of *Half seas over*, may have taken its origin from some such story. They begged us to make a bowl of punch, a liquor they had often heard of, but had never seen. The materials were immediately found, and we succeeded so well, that they preferred it to all the wines on the table, of which they had a great variety. We were obliged to
replenish

replenifh the bowl fo often, that I really expected to fee moft of them under the table. They called it Pontio, and fpoke loudly in its praife; declaring that Pontio (alluding to Pontius Pilate) was a much better fellow than they had ever taken him for. However, after dinner, one of them, a reverend canon, grew excef- fively fick, and while he was throwing up, he turned to me with a rueful coun- tenance, and fhaking his head, he groan- ed out, " Ah, Signor Capitano, fapeva fempre che Pontio era un grande tra- ditore."—" I always knew that Pontius was a great traitor." Another of them overhearing him, exclaimed—" Afpet- tatevi Signor Canonico."—" Not fo faft (faid he) my good Canon."—" Niente al pregiudizio di Signor Pontio, vi prego.— Recordate, che Pontio v'ha fatto un cano- nico;—et Pontio ha fatto fua eccellenza uno Vefcovo—Non fcordatevi mai di voftri amici."

Now

Now what do you think of these reverend fathers of the church? their merit, you will easily perceive, does not consist in fasting and prayer.—Their creed, they say, they have a good deal modernized, and is much simpler than that of Athanasius.—One of them told me, that if we would but stay with them for some little time, we should soon be convinced that they were the happiest fellows on earth. " We have exploded (said he) from our system every thing that is dismal or melancholy; and are persuaded, that of all the roads in the universe, the road to heaven must be the pleasantest and least gloomy : If it be not so, (added he) God have mercy upon us, for I am afraid we shall never get there." I told him I could not flatter him; " That if laughing was really a sin, as some people taught, they were certainly the greatest of all sinners." " Well (said he) we shall at least endeavour to be happy here; and that, I am persuaded, is the best of all preparations

rations for happiness hereafter. Abstinence (continued he) from all innocent and lawful pleasures, we reckon one of the greatest sins, and guard against it with the utmost care: and I am pretty sure it is a sin that none of us here will ever be damned for."—He concluded by repeating two lines, which he told me was their favourite maxim; the meaning of which was exactly those of Mr. Pope,

" For God is paid when man receives,
" To enjoy is to obey."

This is not the first time I have met with this libertine spirit amongst the Roman Catholic clergy. There is so much nonsense and mummery in their worship, that they are afraid lest strangers should believe they are serious; and perhaps too often fly to the opposite extreme.

We were, however, much pleased with the bishop; he is greatly and deservedly respected,

spected, yet his prefence did no wife diminish, but rather increafed the jollity of the company. He entered into every joke, joined in the repartee, at which he is a great proficient, and entirely laid afide his epifcopal dignity; which, however, I am told, he knows very well how to affume when it is neceffary. He placed us next to himfelf, and behaved indeed, in every refpect, with the greateft eafe and politenefs. He is one of the firft families of the ifland, and brother to the Prince of——. I had his whole pedigree pat, but now I have loft it; no matter: he is an honeft, pleafant little fellow, and that is of much more confequence. He is not yet forty; and fo high a promotion in fo early a period of life, is reckoned very extraordinary, this being the richeft bifhoprick in the kingdom. He is a good fcholar, and very deeply read, both in ancient and modern learning; and his genius is in no degree inferior to his erudition. The fimilarity

larity of character and circumstances struck me so strongly, that I could scarce help thinking I had got beside our worthy and respectable friend, the b——p of D———y, which, I assure you, still added greatly to the pleasure I had in his company. I told the bishop of this; adding, that he was brother to l—d B———l: he seemed much pleased, and said, he had often heard of the family, both when lord B—— was ambassador in Spain, and his other brother commander in the Mediterranean.

We found in this company a number of Free Masons, who were delighted beyond measure, when they discovered that we were their brethren. They pressed us to spend a few more days amongst them, and offered us letters to Palermo, and every other town we should think of visiting; but the heats are increasing so violently, that we were afraid of prolonging our expedition, lest we should be caught by the

Sirocc

Sirocc winds, fuppofed to blow from the burning deferts of Africa, and fometimes attended with dangerous confequences to thofe that travel over Sicily.

But I find I have omitted feveral circumftances of our dinner. I fhould have told you, that it was an annual feaft given by the nobility of Agrigentum to the bifhop. It was ferved in an immenfe granary, half full of wheat, on the fea fhore, chofen on purpofe to avoid the heat. The whole was on plate: and what appeared fingular to us, but I believe is a much better method than ours; great part of the fruit was ferved up with the fecond courfe, the firft difh of which that went round was ftrawberries. The Sicilians were a good deal furprifed to fee us eat them with cream and fugar, yet upon trial they did not at all diflike the compofition.

The defert confifted of a great variety of fruits, and ftill a greater of ices: thefe

were

were so disguised in the shapes of peaches, figs, oranges, nuts, &c. that a person unaccustomed to ices might very easily have been taken in, as an honest sea-officer was lately at the house of a certain minister of your acquaintance, not less distinguished for the elegance of his table, than the exact formality and subordination to be observed at it. After the second course was removed, and the ices, in the shape of various fruits and sweetmeats, advanced by way of rear-guard; one of the servants carried the figure of a fine large peach to the captain, who, unacquainted with deceit of any kind, never doubted that it was a real one; and cutting it through the middle, in a moment had one large half of it in his mouth; at first he only looked grave, and blew up his cheeks to give it more room; but the violence of the cold soon getting the better of his patience, he began to tumble it about from side to side in his mouth, his eyes rushing out of water, till at last, able to hold no longer, he ſpit it out upon his plate, exclaiming with a horrid oath, "A painted ſnowball, by G—d!" and wiping away his tears with his napkin, he turned in a rage to the Italian ſervant that had helped him, with a "D—n your maccaroni eyes, you ſon of a b—, what did you mean by that?" —The fellow, who did not underſtand a word of it, could not forbear ſmiling, which ſtill convinced the captain the more that it was a trick; and he was juſt going to throw the reſt of the ſnowball in his face, but was prevented by one of the company; when recovering from his paſſion, and thinking the object unworthy of it, he only added in a ſofter tone, "Very well, neighbour, I only wiſh I had you on board ſhip for half an hour, you ſhould have a dozen before you could ſay Jack Robinſon, for all your painted cheeks."

I aſk pardon for this digreſſion, but as it is a good laughable ſtory, I know you will

will excufe it. About fix o'clock, we took a cordial leave of our jolly friends at Agrigentum; and embarked on board our Sparonaro at the new port. I fhould have told you, that this harbour has lately been made at a very great expence; this city having always been one of the principal ports of the ifland, for the exportation of grain. The bifhop and his company went into a large barge, and failed round the harbour, we faluted them as we went out; they returned the compliment, and we took a fecond leave. The evening was fine, and we coafted along for a good many miles; we paffed feveral points and little promontories, that were exceedingly beautiful and picturefque, many of them were covered with noble large aloes in full blow. In one place, I counted upwards of 200 of thofe fine majeftic plants all in flower; a fight which I imagined was hardly to be met with in the world.—After fun-fet,—alas, fain would I conceal what happened after

after fun-set! but life you know is chequered with good and evil, and it would have been great presumption to receive so much of the one, without expecting a little dash of the other too.—Besides, a sea expedition is nothing without a storm. Our journal would never have been readable, had it not been for this.—Well, I assure you, we had it. It was not indeed so violent as the great one off Louisburgh, or perhaps even that described by Virgil; the reading of which is said to have made people sea-sick; but it was rather too much for our little bark.—I was going to tell you that after sun-set the sky began to over-cast, and in a short time the whole atmosphere appeared fiery and threatening. We attempted to get into some creek, but could find none. The wind grew loud, and we found it was in vain to proceed; but as the night was dark and hazy, we were dubious about the possibility of reaching the port of Agrigentum. How-

However, this was all we had for it, as there were none other within many miles. Accordingly we tacked about, and plying both oars and fail, with great care not to come amongſt the rocks and breakers, in about two hours we ſpied the light-houſe ; by which we directed our courſe, and got ſafely into port, betwixt one and two in the morning : we lay down on our mattraſs; and ſlept found till ten; when finding the falſity of our hypotheſis, that there could be no bad weather in the Mediterranean at this ſeaſon, we unanimouſly agreed to have nothing more to do with Sparonaros, and ſent immediately to engage mules to carry us over the mountains to Palermo. The ſtorm continued with violence the whole day, and made us often thank heaven that we had got ſafely back. It was not till five in the afternoon that we had mules, guides, and guards provided us ; when we ſet off, pretty much in the ſame order, and in the ſame equipage as we had done about three

weeks

weeks ago from Meſſina. Our guards attempted to fill us with the moſt dreadful apprehenſions of this road, ſhewing us every mile, where ſuch a one was robbed, ſuch another was murdered; and entertained us with ſuch melancholy ditties the greateſt part of the way. Indeed, if one half of their ſtories be true, it is certainly the moſt dangerous road in the world; but I looked upon moſt of them as fictions, invented only to increaſe their own conſequence, and to procure a little more money. There is, indeed, ſome foundation for theſe ſtories; as there are numbers of gibbets erected on the road *in terrorem*; and every little baron has the power of life and death in his own domain. Our biſhop's brother, whoſe name I have forgot, ſeized lately four and twenty of thoſe deſperate banditti, after a ſtout reſiſtance, where ſeveral were killed on both ſides; and notwithſtanding that ſome of them were under the protection of the nobility, and in their ſervice,

ſervice, they were all hanged. However, this has by no means rooted them out. Our guards in the ſuſpicious places went with their pieces cock'd, and kept a cloſe look-out to either ſide of them; but we ſaw nothing to alarm us, except the moſt dreadful roads in the world; in many places worſe than any thing I ever met with amongſt the Alps.

After travelling about twenty miles, we arrived by two in the morning at the moſt wretched—I don't know what to call it—there was not any one thing to be had but a little ſtraw for the mules. However, after a good deal of difficulty, we at laſt got fire enough to boil our tea-kettle, and having brought bread from Agrigentum, we made an excellent meal. Our tea-table was a round ſtone in the field, and as the moon ſhone bright, we had no occaſion for any other luminary. You may believe our ſtay here was as ſhort as poſſible; the house was too dreadfully nasty to enter it, and the stable was full of poor wretches sleeping on the bare ground. In short, I never saw in any country so miserable an Inn, for so it is styled. We mounted our cavalry with all expedition, and in a very short time got into the woods, where we were serenaded by the nightingale as we went along, who made us a full apology and atonement for the bad cheer we had met with. In a short time it was day, and then we had entertainment enough from the varied scenes of the most beautiful, wild, and romantic country in the world.—The fertility of many of the plains is truly astonishing, without inclosures, without manure, and almost without culture. It is with reason, that this island was styled " Romani imperii horreum," the granary of the Roman Empire. Were it cultivated, it would still be the great granary of Europe. Pliny says, it yielded a hundred after one; and Diodorus, who was a native of the island,

island, and wrote on the spot, assures us that it produced wheat and other grain spontaneously; and Homer advances the same fact in the Odyssey:

> The soil untill'd, a ready harvest yields,
> With wheat and barley wave the golden fields;
> Spontaneous wines from weighty clusters pour,
> And Jove descends in each prolific shower.
>
> POPE.

Many of the mountains seemed to be formed by subterraneous fire; several of them retain their conical figure and their craters, but not so exact as those on Mount Ætna, as they are probably much older. I likewise observed many pieces of lava on the road, and in the beds of the torrents; and a good deal of the stone called tufa, which is certainly the production of a volcano; so that I have no doubt, that a great part of this island, as well as the neighbouring ones of Lipari, &c. has been originally formed by subterraneous fire: we likewise wife paſſed ſome quarries of a kind of talc; and alſo of a coarſe alabaſter; of this they make a ſort of ſtucco or plaiſter, reſembling that of Paris; but what I much regretted, we miſſed ſeeing the famous ſalt of Agrigentum; found in the earth, about four or five miles from that city. It has this remarkable property different from all other ſalt, that in the fire it preſently melts; but in the water it cracks and ſplits, but never diſſolves. It is celebrated by Pliny, Ariſtotle, and others of the ancient, as well as modern naturaliſts. Fazzello, whom I have brought along with me to read by the road, ſays, he has often experienced this; he adds from the authority of theſe ancient authors, that they formerly had mines of this ſalt, ſo pure and ſolid, that the ſtatuaries and ſculptors preferred it to marble, and made various works of it.

The poor people of the village have found us out, and with looks full of miſery have

have furrounded our door.—Accurfed tyranny,—what defpicable objects we become in thy hands !—Is it not inconceivable, how any government fhould be able to render poor and wretched, a country which produces almoft fpontaneoufly, every thing that even luxury can defire ? But alas ! poverty and wretchednefs have ever attended the Spanifh yoke, both on this, and on t'other fide of the globe.—They make it their boaft that the fun never fets on their dominions, but forget that fince they became fuch, they have left him nothing to fee in his courfe but deferted fields, barren wilderneffes, oppreffed peafants, and lazy, lying, lecherous monks.—Such are the fruits of their boafted conquefts.—They ought rather to be afhamed that ever the fun fhould fee them at all.—The fight of thefe poor people has filled me with indignation. This village is furrounded by the fineft country in the world, yet there was neither bread nor wine to be found in it,

and

and the poor inhabitants appear more than half starved.

"'Mongſt Ceres' richeſt gifts with want oppreſs'd,
"And 'midſt the flowing vineyard, die of thirſt,"

I ſhall now think of concluding, as I do not recollect that I have much more to ſay to you. Beſides, I find myſelf exceeding ſleepy. I ſincerely wiſh it may not be the ſame caſe with you, before you have read thus far. We have ordered our mules to be ready by five o'clock, and ſhall again travel all night;—the heats are too great to allow of it by day; adieu.—Theſe two fellows are ſtill found aſleep. In a few minutes I ſhall be ſo too, for the pen is almoſt dropping out of my hand. Farewell.

SICILY AND MALTA.

LETTER XXI.

Palermo, June 19.

WE are now arrived at the great capital of Sicily, which in our opinion in beauty and elegance is greatly superior to Naples. It is not, indeed, so large, but the regularity, the uniformity and neatness of its streets and buildings, render it much more pleasing; it is full of people, who have mostly an air of affluence and gaiety. And indeed we seem to have got into a new world.—But stop—not so fast.—I had forgot that you have still 50 miles to travel on a cursed stubborn mule, over rocks and precipices; for I can see no reason, why we should bring you at once into all the sweets of Palermo, without bearing at least some little part in

the

the fatigues of the journey. Come, we shall make them as short as possible.

We left you, I think, in a little village on the top of a high mountain. We should indeed use you very ill, were we to leave you there any longer; for I own it is the very worst country quarter, that ever fell to my lot. However, we got a good comfortable sleep in it, the only one thing it afforded us; and the fleas, the bugs, and chickens, did all that lay in their power even to deprive us of that, but we defied them. Our two leaders came to awake us before five, apostrophying their entry with a detail of the horrid robberies and murders that had been committed in the neighbourhood; all of them, you may be sure, on the very road that we were to go.

Our whole squadron was drawn out, and we were ranged in order of battle, by five

five o'clock, when we began our march, attended by the whole village, man, woman, and child. We foon got down amongſt the woods, and endeavoured to forget the objects of miſery we had left behind us. The beauty and richneſs of the country increaſed in proportion as we advanced. The mountains, although of a great height (that we have left, is near 4000 feet, the mercury ſtanding at 26 inches 2 lines), are covered to the very ſummit with the richeſt paſture. The graſs in the valleys is already burnt up, fo that the flocks are all upon the mountains. The gradual ſeparation of heat and cold, is very viſible in taking a view of them. The valleys are brown and ſcorched, and ſo are the mountains to a conſiderable height; they then begin to take a ſhade of green, which grows deeper and deeper, and covers the whole upper region; however, on the ſummit, the graſs and corn are by no means ſo luxuriant as about the middle.

We

We were amazed at the richnefs of the crops, far fuperior to any thing I had ever feen either in England or Flanders, where the happy foil is affifted by all the arts of cultivation; whilft here, the wretched hufbandman can hardly afford to give it a furrow; and gathers in with a heavy heart, the moft luxuriant harveft. To what purpofe is it given him? only to lie a dead weight upon his hand, fometimes till it is entirely loft; exportation being prohibited to all fuch as cannot pay exorbitantly for it to the fovereign.—What a contraft is there betwixt this, and the little uncouth country of Switzerland!—to be fure, the dreadful confequences of opprefion can never be fet in a more ftriking oppofition to the bleffings and charms of liberty. Switzerland, the very excrefcence of Europe, where Nature feems to have thrown out all her cold and ftagnating humours; full of lakes, marfhes, and woods, and furrounded by immenfe rocks, and

and everlasting mountains of ice, the barren, but sacred, ramparts of liberty. Switzerland, enjoying every blessing, where every blessing seems to have been denied; whilst Sicily, covered by the most luxuriant hand of Nature; where Heaven seems to have showered down its richest blessings with the utmost prodigality; groans under the most abject poverty, and with a pale and wan visage, starves in the midst of plenty.—It is liberty alone that works this standing miracle.—Under her plastic hands the mountains sink, the lakes are drained; and these rocks, these marshes, these woods, become so many sources of wealth and of pleasure.—But what has temperance to do with wealth?

" Here reigns Content,
" And Nature's child Simplicity; long since
" Exil'd from polished realms."

" 'Tis Industry supplies
" The little Temperance wants; and rosy Health
" Sits smiling at the board."

You

You will begin to think I am in danger of turning poetical in thefe claffic fields;— I am fure I neither fufpected any of the mountains we have paffed to be Parnaffus; nor did I believe any one of the nine foolifh enough to inhabit them, except Melpomene perhaps, as fhe is fo fond of tragical faces: however, I fhall now get you out of them as foon as poffible, and bring you once more into the gay world; I affure you, I have often wifhed that you could have lent me your mufe, on this expedition; my letters would then have been more worth the reading; but you muft take the will for the deed.

After travelling till about midnight, we arrived at another miferable village, where we flept for fome hours on ftraw, and continued our journey again by day-break. We had the pleafure of feeing the rifing fun from the top of a pretty high mountain, and were delighted with the profpect of

SICILY AND MALTA.

of Strombolo, and the other Lipari iflands, at a great diftance from us. On our defcent from this mountain, we found ourfelves on the banks of the fea, and took that road, preferable to an inland one, although feveral miles nearer. We foon lighted from our mules, and plunged into the water, which has ever made one of our greateft pleafures in this expedition; nobody that has not tried it, can conceive the delight of this; after the fatigue of fuch a journey, and paffing three days without undreffing. Your friend Fullarton, though only feventeen, but whofe mind and body now equally defpife every fatigue, found himfelf ftrong as a lion, and fit to begin fuch another march. We boiled our tea-kettle under a fig-tree, and eat a breakfaft that might have ferved a company of ftrolling players.

The approach to Palermo is fine. The alleys are planted with fruit-trees, and large American aloes in full blow.—Near the city we paffed a place of execution, where the quarters of a number of robbers were hung up upon hooks, like fo many hams; fome of them appeared newly executed, and made a very unfightly figure. On our arrival, we learned that a prieft and three others had been taken a few days ago, after an obftinate defence, in which feveral were killed on both fides; the prieft, rather than fubmit to his conquerors, plunged his hanger into his breaft, and died on the fpot: the reft fubmitted and were executed.

As there is but one inn in Palermo, we were obliged to agree to their own terms (five ducats a day). We are but indifferently lodged; however, it is the only inn we have yet feen in Sicily, and indeed, may be faid to be the only one in the ifland. It is kept by a noify troublefome Frenchwoman, who I find will plague us; there is no keeping her out of our rooms, and
fhe

she never comes in without telling us of such a prince and such a duke, that were so superlatively happy at being lodged in her house: we can easily learn that they were all desperately in love with her; and indeed she seems to take it very much amiss, that we are not inclined to be of the same sentiments. I have already been obliged to tell her, that we are very retired sort of people, and do not like company: I find she does not esteem us the better for it; and this morning, (as I passed through the kitchen, without speaking to her) I overheard her exclaim, " Ah mon Dieu! comme ces Anglois sont " sauvages." I believe we must take more notice of her, otherwise we shall certainly have our rent raised; but she is as fat as a pig, and as ugly as the devil, and lays on a quantity of paint on each of her swelled cheeks, that looks like a great plaister of red Morocco. Her picture is hanging in the room where I am now writing, as well as that of her hufband, who, by the bye, is a ninny: they are no lefs vile curiofities than the originals.—He is drawn with his fnuff-box open in one hand, and a difh of coffee in the other; and at the fame time, *fait l' aimable à Madame.* I took notice of this triple occupation, which feemed to imply fomething particular. She told me that the thought was her's; that her hufband was excceedingly fond of fnuff and of coffee, and wanted by this to fhew that he was ftill more occupied with her than with either of them.—I could not help applauding the ingenuity of the conceit. Madame is painted with an immenfe bouquet in her breaft, and an orange in her right-hand, emblematic of her fweetnefs and purity; and has the prettieft little fmirk on her face you can imagine. She told me that fhe infifted on the painter drawing her *avec le fouris fur le vifage,* but as he had not *efprit* enough to make her fmile naturally, fhe was obliged to force

force one, "qui n'etoit pas tout a fait
" si jolie que le naturel, mais qui vaudroit
" toujours mieux que de parroitre sombre."
I agreed with her perfectly; and assured
her it became her very much, " parceque
" les dames grasses sont toujours de bonne
" humeur."—I found, however, that she
would willingly have excused me the latter
part of the compliment, which more than
lost all that I had gained by the former.
" Il est vrai" (said she, a good deal piqued)
" j'ai un peu de l'em bon point, mais pas
" tant grasse pourtant." I pretended to
excuse myself, from not understanding all
the finesse of the language; and assured
her, that *de l'em bon point* was the very
phrase I meant to make use of. She
accepted the apology, and we are again
reconciled; for, to give the devil his due,
they are good-humoured. She made me a
curtsey, and repeated, " Oui, Monsieur,
" pour parler comme il faut, il faut dire

" *de l'em bon point.*—On ne dit pas graffe."
I affured her, bowing to the ground, that the word fhould for ever be rafed from my vocabulary. She left me with a gracious fmile, and a curtfey much lower than the firft; adding, " Je fçavois bien que Monfieur etoit un homme comme il faut;" at the fame time tripping off on her tiptoes, as light as a feather, to fhew me how much I had been miftaken. This woman made me recollect (what I have always obferved) how little the manners of the French are to be changed by their connexion with other nations; allowing none to be in any degree worthy of imitation but their own. Although fhe has now been here thefe twenty years, fhe is ftill as perfectly French, as if fhe had never been without the gates of Paris; and looks upon every woman in Palermo with the utmoft contempt, becaufe they have never feen that capital, nor heard the

SICILY AND MALTA.

the sublime music of its opera. She is likewise (allowing for the difference of rank) an admirable epitome of all French women, whose universal passion has ever been the desire of admiration, and of appearing young: and ever would be, I believe, were they to live to the age of a thousand. Any person that will take a look of the withered death's heads in their public places, covered over with a thick mask of paint, will be convinced of this.—Now, our old ladies, when they get to the wrong side of sixty, generally take a jump up to the borders of fourscore, and appear no less vain of their years than ever they were of their youth. I know some of them, that I am sure are not less happy, nor less contented, nor (I might almost add) less admired with their wrinkles, than ever they were with their dimples. I do not know whether a cheerful old woman, who is willing to appear so, is more respectable, or more estimable; or a withered witch, who fills up every wrinkle with varnish, and at fourscore attempts to give herself the bloom of four-and-twenty, is ridiculous and contemptible:—but as dinner is on the table, I shall leave it to you to determine. Adieu.

LETTER XXII.

Palermo, June 23d.

I SHALL have a great deal to write you about this city; we are every day more delighted with it, and shall leave it with much regret. We have now delivered our letters, in confequence of which we are loaded with civilities, and have got into a very agreeable fet of acquaintance.—But I shall firft attempt to give you fome little idea of the town, and then fpeak of its inhabitants. It is by much the moft regular I have feen, and is built upon that plan, which I think all large cities ought to follow. The two great ftreets interfect each other in the centre of the city, where they form a handfome fquare, called the Ottangolo, adorned with elegant uniform buildings. From the centre of this fquare, square, you see the whole of these noble streets, and the four great gates of the city which terminate them; the symmetry and beauty of which produce a fine effect. The whole of these are to be magnificently illuminated some time next month, and must certainly be the finest sight in the world. The four gates are each at the distance of about half a mile (the diameter of the city being no more than a mile): these are elegant pieces of architecture richly adorned; particularly the *Porta Nova* and *Porta Felice*, terminating the great street called the *Corso*, that runs south west and north east. The lesser streets in general run parallel to these great ones; so that from every part of the city, in a few minutes walking, you are sure to arrive at one of the capital streets. The *Porte Felice* (by much the handsomest of these gates) opens to the *Marino*, a delightful walk, which constitutes one of the great pleasures of the nobility of Palermo.

It

It is bounded on one fide by the wall of the city, and on the other by the fea, from whence, even at this fcorching feafon, there is always an agreeable breeze. In the centre of the Marino they have lately erected an elegant kind of temple, which, during the fummer months, is made ufe of as an orcheftra for mufic; and as in this feafon they are obliged to convert the night into day, the concert does not begin till the clock ftrikes midnight, which is the fignal for the fymphony to ftrike up: at that time the walk is crowded with carriages and people on foot; and the better to favour pleafure and intrigue, there is an order, that no perfon, of whatever quality, fhall prefume to carry a light with him. The flambeaux are extinguifhed at the Porta Felice, where the fervants wait for the return of the carriages; and the company generally continue an hour or two together in utter darknefs; except when the intruding moon, with her horns

and

and her chaftity comes to difturb them. The concert finifhes about two in the morning, when, for the moft part, every hufband goes home to his own wife. This is an admirable inftitution, and never produces any fcandal: no hufband is fuch a brute as to deny his wife the Marino; and the ladies are fo cautious and circumfpect on their fide, that the more to avoid giving offence, they very often put on mafques.

Their other amufements confift chiefly in their *Converfaziones*, of which they have a variety every night. There is one general one, fupported by the fubfcription of the nobility, which is open every evening at fun-fet, and continues till midnight, when the Marino begins. It better deferves the name of a converfation than any I have feen in Italy; for here the people really come to converfe, whereas in Italy, they only go to play at cards and eat ices. I have

have obferved, that feldom or never one half of the company is engaged in play, nor do they either play long or deep. There are a number of apartments belonging to this converfation, illuminated with wax lights, and kept exceedingly cool and agreeable; and it is indeed altogether one of the moft fenfible and comfortable inftitutions I have feen: befides this, there are generally a number of particular converfations every night, and what will a good deal furprife you, thefe are always held in the apartments of the lying-in ladies; for in this happy climate, childbearing is divefted of all its terrors, and is only confidered as a party of pleafure. This circumftance we were ignorant of till t'other morning. The duke of Verdura, who does us the honours of the place, with great attention and politenefs, came to tell us, we had a vifit to make, that was indifpenfable. " The Princefs Paterno
" (faid

" (said he) was brought to bed last night;
" and it is absolutely incumbent on you
" to pay your respects to her this even-
" ing." At first I thought he was in joke, but he assured me he was serious, and that it would be looked upon as a great unpoliteness to neglect it.—Accordingly we went about sun-set, and found the princess sitting up in her bed, in an elegant undress, with a number of her friends around her. She talked as usual, and seemed to be perfectly well. This conversation is repeated every night during her convalescence, which generally lasts for about eleven or twelve days. This custom is universal, and as the ladies here are very prolific, there are for the most part three or four of these assemblies going on in the city at the same time; possibly the Marino may not a little contribute towards them.

The

The Sicilian ladies marry at thirteen or fourteen, and are sometimes grandmothers before they are thirty.—The Count Stetela presented us a few days ago to his cousin, the Princess Partana, who he told us had a great number of children, the eldest of which was a very fine girl of fifteen. We talked to the princess for half an hour, not in the least doubting all the time that she was the daughter, till at last the young lady came in; and even then, it was not easy to say which appeared the handsomest or the youngest. This lady has had twelve children, and is still in her bloom; she assured me that she never enjoyed more perfect health than when she was in child-bed;—that during the time of her pregnancy she was often indisposed, but that immediately on delivery she was cured of all her complaints, and was capable of enjoying the company of her friends even more than at any other time. I expressed my surprise at this very singular happiness of their climate

mate or conſtitutions; but ſhe appeared ſtill more ſurpriſed when I told her that we loſt many of our fineſt women in childbed, and that even the moſt fortunate and eaſy deliveries were attended with violent pain and anguiſh.—She lamented the fate of our ladies, and thanked Heaven that ſhe was born a Sicilian.

What this ſingularity is owing to, let the learned determine; but it is ſurely one of the capital bleſſings of theſe climates, where the curſe that was laid upon mother Eve ſeems to be entirely taken off: I don't know how the ladies here have deſerved this exemption, as they have at leaſt as much both of Eve and the ſerpent as ours have, and ſtill retain their appetite, as ſtrong as ever, for forbidden fruit.—It ſeems hard, that in our own country, and in Switzerland, where the women in general are the chaſteſt in Europe, that this curſe ſhould fall the heavieſt: it is probably owing to the

the climate:—In cold, but more particularly in mountainous countries, births are difficult and dangerous; in warm and low places they are more eafy; the air of the firft hardens and contracts the fibres, that of the fecond foftens and relaxes them. In fome places in Switzerland, and amongft the Alps, they lofe almoft one half of their women in childbed, and thofe that can afford it, often go down to the low countries fome weeks before they lie in, and find their deliveries much eafier. One may eafily conceive what a change it muft make upon the whole frame, to add the preffure of a column of air of two or three thoufand feet more than it is accuftomed to: and if mufcular motion is performed by the preffure of the atmofphere, as fome have alleged, how much muft this add to the action of every mufcle!—However, if this hypothefis were true, our ftrength fhould have been diminifhed one third on the top of Ætna, which did not appear to be the cafe;

case; as we had passed through one third of the quantity of air of the whole atmosphere. I have often thought that physicians pay too little attention to these considerations; and that in skilful hands they might be turned to great account, in the cure of many diseases: they only send their patients to such a degree of latitude, but never think of the degree of altitude in the atmosphere. Thus, people with the same complaints are sent to Aix and to Marseilles, although the air in these two places must be essentially different. Marseilles is on the level of the sea, and Aix (as I myself measured it) is near 600 feet above it.— Now I am persuaded, that in such a country as Switzerland, or on such a mountain as Ætna, where it is easy at all times to take off a pressure from the human body of many thousand pounds weight, that an ingenious physician might make great discoveries; nor indeed would these discoveries be confined to the changing of the quantity

of

of air that presses on the body, but would likewise be extended to the changing of the quality of the air we breathe; which, on the side of Ætna, or any very high mountain, is more varied than in travelling through fifty degrees of latitude. I beg pardon for this digression; the only amends I can make, is to put it out of my power to trouble you with any more, and thus abruptly assure you how much, &c.

LETTER XXIII.

Palermo, June 26th.

OUR fondness for Palermo increases every day, and we are beginning to look forward with regret to the time of our leaving it, which is now fast approaching. We have made acquaintance with many sensible and agreeable people. The Sicilians appear frank and sincere; and their politeness does not consist in show and grimace, like some of the polite nations of the continent. The viceroy sets the pattern of hospitality, and he is followed by the rest of the nobles. He is an amiable, agreeable man, and I believe is as much beloved and esteemed as a viceroy to an absolute monarch can be. He was in England in his youth, and is still fond of many of our authors, with whom he seems

to

SICILY AND MALTA.

to be intimately acquainted; he speaks the language tolerably well, and encourages the learning of it amongst his people.—He may be considered with regard to Naples, as what the lord lieutenant of Ireland is with regard to England, with this trifling difference, that, like his master, he is invested with absolute authority; and keeps his parliament (for he has one too) in the most perfect subjection. The patriots here, although a very numerous body, have never been able to gain one point, no nor a place, nor even a pension for a needy friend. Had lord Townshend the power of the marquis Fogliano, I suppose your Hibernian squabbles (of which we hear so much, even at this distant corner) would soon have an end.—Notwithstanding this great authority, he is affable and familiar, and makes his house agreeable to every body. We go very often to his assemblies, and have dined with him several times; his table is served with elegance and magnificence, much superior indeed to that of his Sicilian majesty, who eats off a service of plate, at least 300 years old, very black and rusty indeed: I heard a gentleman ask one day, whilst we were standing round the table, if it had not been dug out of Herculaneum. That of the viceroy is very elegant, and indeed the whole of his entertainments correspond with it; though we have as yet seen nothing here, to be compared to the luxury of our feast in the granary at Agrigentum.

The Sicilian cookery is a mixture of the French and Spanish; and the Olio still preserves its rank and dignity in the centre of the table, surrounded by a numerous train of fricassees, fricandeaus, ragouts, and pet de loups; like a grave Spanish Don, amidst a number of little smart marquis.—The other nobility, whom we have had occasion to see, are likewise very magnificent in their entertainments; but most particularly in in their deferts and ices, of which there is a greater variety than I have feen in any other country. They are very temperate with regard to wine; though, fince we have taught them our method of toafting ladies they are fond of, and of hob and nobing with their friends, ringing the two glaffes together; this focial practice has animated them fo much, that they have been fometimes led to drink a greater quantity than they are accuftomed to; and they often reproach us with having made them drunkards. In their ordinary living they are very frugal and temperate; and from the fobriety we have feen here, we are now more perfuaded that the elevated fituation of Agrigentum muft be one great caufe of its drunkennefs.

The Sicilians have always had the character of being very amorous, and furely not without reafon. The whole nation are poets, even the peafants; and a man ftands a poor chance for a miſtreſs, that is not capable of celebrating her praiſes. I believe it is generally allowed that the paſtoral poetry had its origin in this iſland; and Theocritus, after whom they ſtill copy, will ever be looked upon as the prince of paſtoral poets. And indeed in muſic too, as well as poetry, the ſoft, amorous pieces are generally ſtyled *Siciliani*; theſe they uſed to play all night under their miſtreſſes' windows, to expreſs the delicacy of their paſſion; but ſerenading is not now ſo much in faſhion, as it was during the time of their more intimate connexion with Spain, when it was ſaid by one of their authors, that no perſon could paſs for a man of gallantry that had not got a cold; and was ſure never to ſucceed in making love, unleſs he made it in a hoarſe voice. The ladies are not now ſo rigid, and will ſometimes condeſcend to hear a man, even although he ſhould ſpeak in a clear tone.— Neither do they any longer require the prodigious

prodigious martial feats, that were then neceſſary to win them.—The attacking of a mad bull, or a wild boar, was reckoned the handſomeſt compliment a lover could pay to his miſtreſs; and the putting theſe animals to death ſoftened her heart much more than all the ſighing love-ſick tales that could be invented. This has been humorouſly ridiculed by one of their poets. He ſays that Cupid's little golden dart was now changed into a maſſy ſpear, which anſwered a double purpoſe; for at the ſame time that it pierced the tough bull's hide, it likewiſe pierced the tender lady's heart.— But theſe Gothic cuſtoms are now confined to Spain, and the gentle Sicilians have re-aſſumed their ſoftneſs. To tell you the truth, gallantry is pretty much upon the ſame footing here as in Italy, the eſtabliſhment of Ciccisbees is pretty general, though not quite ſo univerſal as on the continent. However, a breach of the marriage vow is no longer looked upon as one of the deadly ſins; and

and the confeffors fall upon eafy and pleafant enough methods of making them atone for it. The hufbands are content; and like able generals, make up for the lofs of one fortrefs, by the taking of another. However, female licentioufnefs has by no means come to fuch a height as in Italy. We have feen a great deal of domeftic happinefs; hufbands and wives that truly love one another, and whofe mutual care and pleafure is the education of their children. I could name a number;—the Duke of Verdura, the Prince Partana, the Count Bufcemi, and many others who live in the moft facred union. Such fights are very rare on the continent. But indeed the ftyle that young people are brought up in here, feems to lay a much more folid foundation for matrimonial happinefs, than either in France or Italy. The young ladies are not fhut up in convents till the day of their marriage, but for the moft part live in the houfe with their parents, where they

they receive their education, and are every day in company with their friends and relations. From what I can obferve, I think they are allowed almoft as much liberty as with us. In their great affemblies we often fee a club of young people (of both fexes) get together in a corner, and amufe themfelves for hours, at crofs purpofes or fuch like games, without the mothers being under the leaft anxiety; indeed, we fometimes join in thefe little parties, and find them extremely entertaining. In general, they are quick and lively, and have a number of thofe *jeux d'efprit*, which I think muft ever be a proof, in all countries, of the familiar intercourfe betwixt the young people of the two fexes; for all thefe games are infipid, if they are not feafoned by fomething of that invifible and fubtile agency, which renders every thing more interefting in thefe mixed focieties, than in the lifelefs ones, compofed of only one part of the fpecies. Thus, in Italy, Spain,

Spain, and Portugal, I have never feen any of thefe games; in France feldom, but in Switzerland, (where the greateft liberty and familiarity are enjoyed amongft the young people) they are numberlefs.——— But the converfation hour is arrived, and our carriage is waiting.

Adieu.

LETTER XXIV.

Palermo, June 28th.

THERE are two small countries, one to the east, the other to the west of this city, where the principal nobility have their country palaces. Both these we have visited; there are many noble houses in each of them. That to the east is called La Bagaria, that to the west Il Colle.—We are this instant returned from La Bagaria, and I hasten to give you an account of the ridiculous things we have seen, though perhaps you will not thank me for it.

The palace of the Prince of Valguanera is, I think, by much the finest and most beautiful of all the houses of the Bagaria; but it is far from being the most extraordinary: were I to describe it, I should only tell you of things you have often seen and heard of

in

in other countries, so I shall only speak of one, which, for its singularity, certainly is not to be paralleled on the face of the earth; it belongs to the prince of P———, a man of immense fortune, who has devoted his whole life to the study of monsters and chimeras, greater and more ridiculous than ever entered into the imagination of the wildest writers of romance or knight-errantry.

The amazing crowd of statues that surround his house, appear at a distance like a little army drawn up for its defence; but when you get amongst them, and every one assumes his true likeness, you imagine you have got into the regions of delusion and enchantment; for of all that immense group, there is not one made to represent any object in nature; nor is the absurdity of the wretched imagination that created them less astonishing than its wonderful fertility. It would require a volume to defcribe the whole, and a fad volume indeed it would make. He has put the heads of men to the bodies of every fort of animal, and the heads of every other animal to the bodies of men. Sometimes he makes a compound of five or fix animals that have no fort of refemblance in nature. He puts the head of a lion to the neck of a goofe, the body of a lizard, the legs of a goat, the tail of a fox. On the back of this monfter, he puts another, if poffible ftill more hideous, with five or fix heads, and a bufh of horns, that beats the beaft in the Revelations all to nothing. There is no kind of horn in the world that he has not collected; and his pleafure is to fee them all flourifhing upon the fame head. This is a ftrange fpecies of madnefs; and it is truly unaccountable that he has not been fhut up many years ago; but he is perfectly innocent, and troubles nobody by the indulgence of his phrenzy; on the

contrary,

contrary, he gives bread to a number of ſtatuaries and other workmen, whom he rewards in proportion as they can bring their imaginations to coincide with his own; or, in other words, according to the hideouſneſs of the monſters they produce. It would be idle and tireſome to be particular in an account of theſe abſurdities. The ſtatues that adorn, or rather deform the great avenue, and ſurround the court of the palace, amount already to 600, notwithſtanding which, it may be truly ſaid, that he has not broke the ſecond commandment; for of all that number, there is not the likeneſs of any thing in heaven above, in the earth beneath, or in the waters under the earth. The old ornaments which were put up by his father, who was a ſenſible man, appear to have been in a good taſte. They have all been knocked to pieces, and laid together in a heap, to make room for this new creation.

The infide of this inchanted caftle correfponds exactly with the out; it is in every refpect as whimfical and fantaftical, and you cannot turn yourfelf to any fide, where you are not ftared in the face by fome hideous figure or other. Some of the apartments are fpacious and magnificent, with high arched roofs; which inftead of plaifter or ftucco, are compofed entirely of large mirrors, nicely joined together. The effect that thefe produce (as each of them make a fmall angle with the other) is exactly that of a multiplying glafs; fo that when three or four people are walking below, there is always the appearance of three or four hundred walking above. The whole of the doors are likewife covered over with fmall pieces of mirror, cut into the moft ridiculous fhapes, and intermixed with a great variety of cryftal and glafs of different colours. All the chimney-pieces, windows, and fide-boards are crowded with pyramids and pillars of tea-pots, caudle-

caudle-cups, bowls, cups, saucers, &c. strongly cemented together; some of these columns are not without their beauty: one of them has a large china chamber-pot for its base, and a circle of pretty little flower-pots for its capital; the shaft of the column, upwards of four feet long, is composed entirely of tea-pots of different sizes, diminished gradually from the base to the capital. The profusion of china that has been employed in forming these columns is incredible; I dare say there is not less than forty pillars and pyramids formed in this strange fantastic manner.

Most of the rooms are paved with fine marble tables of different colours, that look like so many tomb-stones. Some of these are richly wrought with lapis lazuli, porphyry, and other valuable stones; their fine polish is now gone, and they only appear like common marble; the place of these beautiful tables he has supplied by a new

new set of his own invention, some of which are not without their merit. These are made of the finest tortoise-shell mixed with mother of pearl, ivory, and a variety of metals; and are mounted on fine stands of solid brass.

The windows of this inchanted castle are composed of a variety of glass of every different colour, mixed without any sort of order or regularity. Blue, red, green, yellow, purple, violet.—So that at each window, you may have the heavens and earth of whatever colour you chuse, only by looking through the pane that pleases you.

The house-clock is cased in the body of a statue; the eyes of the figure move with the pendulum, turning up their white and black alternately, and make a hideous appearance.

His bed-chamber and dressing-room are like two apartments in Noah's ark; there is scarce a beast, however vile, that he has not placed there; toads, frogs, serpents, lizards, scorpions, all cut out in marble, of their respective colours. There are a good many busts too, that are not less singularly imagined.—Some of these make a very handsome profile on one side; turn to the other, and you have a skeleton; here you see a nurse with a child in her arms; its back is exactly that of an infant; its face is that of a wrinkled old woman of ninety.

For some minutes one can laugh at these follies, but indignation and contempt soon get the better of your mirth, and the laugh is turned into a sneer. I own I was soon tired of them; though some things are so strangely fancied, that it may well excuse a little mirth, even from the most rigid cynic.

The

The family ftatues are charming; they have been done from fome old pictures, and make a moft venerable appearance; he has dreffed them out from head to foot, in new and elegant fuits of marble; and indeed the effect it produces is more ridiculous than any thing you can conceive. Their fhoes are all of black marble, their ftockings generally of red; their clothes are of different colours, blue, green, and variegated, with a rich lace of *giall' antique*. The periwigs of the men and head-dreffes of the ladies are of fine white; fo are their fhirts, with long flowing ruffles of alabafter. The walls of the houfe are covered with fome fine baffo relievos of white marble, in a good tafte; thefe he could not well take out, or alter, fo he has only added immenfe frames to them. Each frame is compofed of four large marble tables.

The author and owner of this fingular collection is a poor miferable lean figure, fhivering shivering at a breeze, and seems to be afraid of every body he speaks to; but (what surprised me) I have heard him talk speciously enough on several occasions. He is one of the richest subjects in the island, and it is thought he has not laid out less than 20,000 pounds in the creation of this world of monsters and chimeras.—He certainly might have fallen upon some way to prove himself a fool at a cheaper rate. However it gives bread to a number of poor people, to whom he is an excellent master. His house at Palermo is a good deal in the same style; his carriages are covered with plates of brass, so that I really believe some of them are musket proof.

The government have had serious thoughts of demolishing the regiment of monsters he has placed round his house, but as he is humane and inoffensive, and as this would certainly break his heart, they have as yet forborne. However, the seeing of them by by women with child is said to have been already attended with very unfortunate circumstances; several living monsters having been brought forth in the neighbourhood. The ladies complain that they dare no longer take an airing in the Bagaria; that some hideous form always haunts their imagination for some time after: their husbands too, it is said, are as little satisfied with the great variety of horns. Adieu. I shall write you again by next post, as matter multiplies fast upon me in this metropolis.

Ever yours.

LETTER XXV.

Palermo, June 30th.

THE account the people here give of the Sirocc, or South-east wind, is truly wonderful; to-day, at the viceroy's, we were complaining of the violence of the heat, the thermometer being at 79.— They assured us, that if we staid till the end of next month, we should probably look on this as pleasant cool weather; adding, that if we had once experienced the Sirocc, all other weather will appear temperate.—I asked to what degree the thermometer commonly rose during this wind; but found to my surprise, that there was no such instrument in use amongst them: however, the violence of it, they assure us, is incredible; and that those who had remained many years in Spain and

and Malta, had never felt any heat in thofe countries to compare to it.—How it happens to be more violent in Palermo than in any other part of Sicily, is a myftery that ftill remains to be unfolded. Several treatifes have been written on this fubject, but none that give any tolerable degree of fatisfaction. As we fhall ftay for fome time longer, it is poffible we may have an opportunity of giving you fome account of it.

They have begun fome weeks ago to make preparations for the great feaft of St. Rofolia; and our friends here fay they are determined that we fhall not leave them till after it is over; but this I am afraid will not be in our power. The warm feafon advances, and the time we appointed for our return to Naples is already elapfed; but indeed, return when we will, we fhall make but a bad exchange; and were it not for thofe of our own

own country whom we have left behind us, we certainly fhould have determined on a much longer ftay. But although the fociety here is fuperior to that of Naples, yet,—call it prejudice—or call it what you will, there is a—*je ne fçai quoi,*—a certain confidence in the character, the worth and friendfhip of our own people, that I have feldom felt any where on the continent, except in Switzerland. This fenfation, which conftitutes the charm of fociety, and can alone render it fupportable for any time, is only infpired by fomething analogous, and fympathetic, in our feelings and fentiments ; like two inftruments that are in unifon, and vibrate to each other's touch : for fociety is a concert, and if the inftruments are not in tune, there never can be harmony; and (to carry on the metaphor) this harmony too muft fometimes be heightened and fupported by the introduction of a difcord ; but where difcords predominate,

which

which is often the case between an English and an Italian mind, the music must be wretched indeed.—Had we but a little mixture of our own society, how gladly should we spend the winter in Sicily; but we often think with regret on Mr. Hamilton's and Mr. Walter's families; and wish again to be on the continent.—Indeed, even the pleasures we enjoy here, we owe principally to Mr. Hamilton: his recommendations we have ever found to be the best passport and introduction; and the zeal and cordiality with which these are always received, proceeds evidently not from motives of deference and respect to the minister, but of love and affection to the man.

This morning we went to see a celebrated convent of Capuchins, about a mile without the city; it contains nothing very remarkable but the burial-place, which indeed is a great curiosity. This is a
vast

vaſt ſubterraneous apartment, divided into large commodious galleries, the walls on each ſide of which are hollowed into a variety of niches, as if intended for a great collection of ſtatues; theſe niches, inſtead of ſtatues, are all filled with dead bodies, ſet upright upon their legs, and fixed by the back to the inſide of the nich: their number is about three hundred: they are all dreſſed in the clothes they uſually wore, and form a moſt reſpectable and venerable aſſembly. The ſkin and muſcles, by a certain preparation, become as dry and hard as a piece of ſtock-fiſh; and although many of them have been here upwards of two hundred and fifty years, yet none are reduced to ſkeletons; the muſcles, indeed, in ſome appear to be a good deal more ſhrunk than in others; probably becauſe theſe perſons had been more extenuated at the time of their death.

Here

Here the people of Palermo pay daily viſits to their deceaſed friends, and recal with pleaſure and regret the ſcenes of their paſt life : here they familiarize themſelves with their future ſtate, and chuſe the company they would wiſh to keep in the other world. It is a common thing to make choice of their nich, and to try if their body fits it, that no alterations may be neceſſary after they are dead; and ſometimes, by way of a voluntary penance, they accuſtom themſelves to ſtand for hours in theſe niches.

The bodies of the princes and firſt nobility are lodged in handſome cheſts or trunks, ſome of them richly adorned : theſe are not in the ſhape of coffins, but all of one width, and about a foot and a half, or two feet deep. The keys are kept by the neareſt relations of the family, who

who sometimes come and drop a tear over their departed friends.

I am not sure if this is not a better method of disposing of the dead than ours. These visits must prove admirable lessons of humility; and I assure you, they are not such objects of horror as you would imagine: they are said, even for ages after death, to retain a strong likeness to what they were when alive; so that, as soon as you have conquered the first feeling excited by these venerable figures, you only consider this as a vast gallery of original portraits, drawn after the life, by the justest and most unprejudiced hand. It must be owned that the colours are rather faded; and the pencil does not appear to have been the most flattering in the world; but no matter, it is the pencil of truth, and not of a mercenary, who only wants to please.

We were alleging too, that it might be made of very confiderable utility to fociety; and that thefe dumb orators could give the moft pathetic lectures upon pride and vanity. Whenever a fellow began to ftrut, like Mr. B. or to affect the haughty fupercilious air, he fhould be fent to converfe with his friends in the gallery; and if their arguments did not bring him to a proper way of thinking, I would give him up as incorrigible.

At Bologna they fhewed us the fkeleton of a celebrated beauty, who died at a period of life when fhe was ftill the object of univerfal admiration. By way of making atonement for her own vanity, fhe bequeathed herfelf as a monument, to curb the vanity of others. Recollecting on her death-bed the great adulation that had been paid to her charms, and the fatal change they were foon to undergo, fhe
ordered

ordered that her body should be dissected, and her bones hung up for the inspection of all young maidens who are inclined to be vain of their beauty. However, if she had been preserved in this moral gallery, the lesson would have been stronger; for those very features that had raised her vanity would still have remained, only divested of all their power, and disarmed of every charm.

Some of the Capuchins sleep in these galleries every night, and pretend to have many wonderful visions and revelations; but the truth is, that very few people believe them.

No woman is ever admitted into this convent either dead or alive; and this interdiction is written in large characters over the gate. The poor indolent Capuchins, the frailest of all flesh, have great need

need of such precautions: they have no occupation from without, and they have no resources within themselves, so that they must be an easy prey to every temptation: Bocaccio, and all the books of that kind, are filled with stories of their frailty.—Yesterday, dining at the Prince of Sperlinga's, and talking on this subject, the Abbe T—— gave us an anecdote of a friend of his, who was formerly a brother of this convent. He is known by the name of Fra Pasqual, and has passed through many singular scenes of life, which it would be too long to recount. His last migration, or, if you will, transmigration, was from one of the banditti of this kingdom, in which capacity, he had been enrolled for some time; but, tired of the danger and fatigue to which he was perpetually exposed, he at last determined to exchange the character of the hero, for that of the saint, and try if it was not both safer and surer, to rely on the weakness of others, than on our own strength.

Fra Pasqual pretended a strong compunction for the transgressions of his past life, and made a promise to the Virgin, that the remainder of it should be spent in mortification and penance, to atone for them. To this end, Pasqual, took the vows of poverty and of chastity, and entered into all the rigours of the monastic life.— For some weeks he behaved in a most exemplary manner; he went barefooted, wore a large rosary, and a thicker cord of discipline than any monk in the convent; and his whole deportment gave testimony of the most unfeigned repentance; however, the devil was still at work in the heart of Pasqual, and all these external mortifications only made him work the harder; in short, he found it impossible to drive him out: Pasqual was sensible of this;

this; and afraid left the enemy should at last get the better of him, he thought it adviseable to leave at Palermo the character of sanctity he had acquired, and begin somewhere else upon a new score. He embarked for Naples, where he was soon admitted into a capuchin convent.

As Pasqual knew from experience that the dull uniformity of the monastic life required some little amusements to render it supportable, the first thing he set about was to find a mistress. He made love to a lady of easy virtue, who soon admitted his addresses, but at the same time informed him that he had a formidable rival, who was jealous as a tiger, and would not fail to put them both to death, should he discover the intrigue. This was no other than a lifeguard-man, a fellow of six feet two inches, with a vast spada, like that of Goliah, and a monstrous pair of curled whiskers, that would have caſt a damp on the heart of any man but Fra Paſqual; but the monaſtic life had not yet enervated him; he was accuſtomed to danger, and loved a few difficulties: however, as in his preſent character he could not be on a footing with his rival, he thought it beſt only to make uſe of prudence and ſtratagem to ſupplant him: theſe are the eccleſiaſtical arms, and they have generally been found too hard for the military.

The lady promiſed him an interview as ſoon as the court ſhould go to Portici, where the lifeguard-man's duty obliged him to attend the king. Paſqual waited with impatience for ſome time; at laſt the wiſhed-for night arrived; the king ſet off, after the opera, with all his guards. Paſqual flew like lightning to the arms of his miſtreſs; the preliminaries were ſoon ſettled, and the happy lovers had juſt fallen aſleep, when they were ſuddenly alarmed

alarmed by a rap and a well-known voice at the door. The lady ſtarted up in an agony of deſpair, aſſuring Paſqual that they were both undone; that this was her lover; and if ſome expedient was not fallen upon, in the firſt tranſports of his fury, he would certainly put them both to death. There was no time for reflection; the lifeguard-man demanded entrance in the moſt peremptory manner, and the lady was obliged to inſtant compliance. Paſqual had juſt time to gather his rags together, and cram himſelf in below the bed; at that inſtant the door opened, and the giant came in, rattling his arms and ſtorming at his miſtreſs, for having made him wait ſo long; however, ſhe ſoon pacified him. He then ordered her to ſtrike a light, that he might ſee to undreſs: —this ſtruck Paſqual to the ſoul, and he gave himſelf up for loſt; however, the lady's addreſs ſaved him, when he leaſt expected it. In bringing the tinder, ſhe

took care to let fall some water into the box; and all the beating she and her lover could beat, they could not produce one spark. Every stroke of the flint sounded in Pasqual's ears like his death-knell; but when he heard the lifeguard-man swearing at the tinder for not kindling, he began to conceive some hopes, and blessed the fertile invention of woman.—The lady told him he might easily get a light at the guard, which was at no great distance. —Pasqual's heart leaped with joy;—but when the soldier answered that he was absent without leave, and durst not be seen, it again began to flag; but on his ordering *her* to go—it died within him, and he now found himself in greater danger than ever. The lady herself was disconcerted; but quickly recovering, she told him, it would be too long before she could get dressed; but advised him to go to the corner of a neighbouring street, where there was a lamp burning before
the

the Virgin Mary, who could have no objection to his lighting a candle at it.—Pafqual revived; but the foldier declared he was too much fatigued with his walk, and would rather undrefs in the dark; he at the fame time began to grope below the bed for a bottle of liqueurs, which he knew ftood there.—Pafqual fhook like a quaker, —however, ftill he efcaped.—The lady obferving what he was about, made a fpring, and got him the bottle, at the very inftant he was within an inch of feizing Pafqual's head.—The lady then went to bed, and told her lover, as it was a cold night, fhe would warm his place for him. Pafqual admired her addrefs, and began to conceive fome hopes of efcaping.

His fituation was the moft irkfome in the world; the bed was fo low, that he had no room to move; and when the great heavy lifeguard-man entered it, he found

found himself squeezed down to the ground. He lay trembling and stifling his breath for some time, but found it absolutely impossible to support his situation till morning; and indeed, if it had, his clothes, which were scattered about, must infallibly discover him: he therefore began to think of making his escape; but he could not move without alarming his rival, who was now lying above him. At first he thought of rushing suddenly out, and throwing himself into the street; but this he disdained, and, on second thoughts, determined to seize the lifeguard-man's sword, and either put him to death, or make an honourable capitulation both for himself and the lady. In the midst of these reflections, his rival began to snore, and Pasqual declares that no music was ever so grateful to his soul. He tried to stir a little, and finding that it did not awake the enemy, he by degrees worked himself out of his prison. He immediately laid hold

hold of the great fpada;—when all his fears forfook him, and he felt as bold as a lion. He now relinquifhed the daftardly fcheme of efcaping, and only thought how he could beft retaliate on his rival, for all that he had made him fuffer.

As Pafqual was ftark naked, it was no more trouble to him to put on the foldier's clothes than his own; and as both his cloak and his cappouch together were not worth a fixpence, he thought it moft eligible to equip himfelf à la militaire, and to leave his facerdotal robes to the foldier. In a fhort time he was dreffed cap-a-pie. His greafy cowl, his cloak, his fandals, his rofary, and his rope of difcipline, he gathered together, and placed on a chair before the bed; and girding himfelf with a great buff belt, inftead of the cordon of St. Francis, and grafping his trufty Toledo inftead of the crucifix, he fallied forth into the ftreet. He pondered for fome some time what scheme to fall upon; and at first thought of returning in the character of another lifeguard-man, pretending to have been sent by the officer with a guard in quest of his companion, who not being found in his quarters, was supposed to have deserted: and thus, after having made him pay heartily for all that he had suffered under the bed, to leave him to the enjoyment of his pannic, and the elegant suit of clothes he had provided him. However, he was not satisfied with this revenge, and determined on one still more solid. He went to the guard, and told the officer that he had met a Capuchin friar, with all the ensigns of his sanctity about him, sculking through the streets, in the dead of night, when they pretend to be employed in prayer for the sins of mankind. That prompted by curiosity to follow him, the holy friar as he expected went straight to the house of a celebrated courtezan, that he saw him admitted,

admitted, and liftened at the window till he heard them go to bed together: that if he did not find this information to be true, he fhould refign himfelf his prifoner, and fubmit to whatever punifhment he fhould think proper.

The officer and his guard delighted to have fuch a hold of a Capuchin, (who pretend to be the very models of fanctity, and who revile in a particular manner the licentious life of the military) turned out with the utmoft alacrity, and, under the conduct of Pafqual, furrounded the lady's houfe. Pafqual began thundering at the door; and demanded entrance for the officer and his guard. The unhappy foldier waking with the noife, and not doubting that it was a detachment fent to feize him, gave himfelf up to defpair, and inftantly took fhelter in the very place that Pafqual had fo lately occupied; at the fame time laying hold of all the things he found

found on the chair, never doubting that they were his own clothes. As the lady was fomewhat dilatory in opening the door, Pafqual pretended to put his foot to it, when up it flew, and entering with the officer and his guard, demanded the body of a Capuchin friar, who they were informed lodged with her that night. The lady had heard Pafqual go out, and having no fufpicion that he would inform againſt himſelf, ſhe proteſted her innocence in the moſt ſolemn manner, taking all the ſaints to witneſs that ſhe knew no ſuch perſon: but Pafqual fufpecting the retreat of the lover, began groping below the bed, and foon pulled out his own greaſy cowl and cloak;—" Here (faid he to the officer)— " here are proofs enough:—I'll anfwer for " it, *Signor Padre* himſelf is at no great " diſtance."—And putting his noſe below the bed;—" Fogh (ſay he) I ſmell him;— " he ſtinks like a fox. The fureſt method " of finding a Capuchin, is by the noſe;
" you

" you may wind him a mile off."—Then lowering their lanthorn, they beheld the unfortunate lover fqueezed in betwixt the bed and the ground, and almoft ftifled.— " *Ecco lo*, (faid Pafqual) here he is, with " all the enfigns of his holinefs;" and pulling them out one by one,—the crucifix, the rofary, and the cord of difcipline,— " You may fee (faid he) that the reverend " father came here to do penance :"—and taking up the cord,—" Suppofe now we " fhould affift him in this meritorious " work. *Andiamo, Signor Padre,—an-* " *diamo.*—We will fave you the trouble of " inflicting it yourfelf;—and whether you " came here to fin, or to repent, by your " own maxims, you know, a little found " difcipline is healthful to the foul."—The guard were lying round the bed, in convulfions of laughter; and began breaking the moft galling and moft infolent jokes upon the fuppofed padre.—The lifeguard-
man

man thought himself enchanted.—He at
laft ventured to fpeak, and declared they
were all in a miftake:—that he was no
Capuchin:—upon which the laugh re-
doubled, and the coarfeft jokes were repeated. The lady, in the mean time,
with the beft diffembled marks of fear and
aftonifhment, ran about the room, exclaiming—" *Oime Siamo perduti,—Siamo
incantati,—Siamo inforcelati.*"—Pafqual
delighted to fee that his plan had taken its
full effect, thought it now time to make
his retreat, before the unfortunate lover
could have an opportunity of examining
his clothes, and perhaps detecting him: he
therefore pretended regimental bufinefs,
and regretting much that he was obliged to
join his corps, took leave of the officer and
his guard; at the fame time recommending
by all means, to treat the holy father with
all that reverence and refpect that was due
to fo facred a perfon.

The

The lifeguard-man, when he got out from below the bed, began to look about for his clothes; but obferving nothing but the greafy weeds of a Capuchin friar, he was now perfectly convinced, that Heaven had delivered him over, for his offences, to the power of fome dæmon; (for of all mortals, the Neapolitan foldiers are the moft fuperftitious)---The lady too, acted her part fo well, that he had no longer any doubt of it.---" Thus it is (faid he in a penitential voice) to offend heaven!---I
" own my fin.---I knew it was Friday, and
" yet---O, flefh, flefh!---Had it been any
" other day, I ftill fhould have remained
" what I was.----O, St. Gennaro! I pafs'd
" thee * too without paying the due
" refpect :---thy all-feeing eye has found
" me out. Gentlemen, do with me what
" you pleafe;---I am not what I feem to

---

* A celebrated ftatue of St. Januarius, betwixt Portici and Naples.

I   " be."

" be."———" No, no, (said the officer) we
" are sensible of that.—But, come, Signor
" Padre, on with your garments, and
" march;—we have no time to trifle.——
" Here, Corporal---(giving him the cordon)
" tie his hands, and let him feel the weight
" of St. Francis.---The saint owes him that,
" for having so impudently denied him for
" his master."---The poor soldier was perfectly passive;——they arrayed him in the sandals, the cowl, and the cloak of Fra Pasqual, and put the great rosary about his neck; and a most woeful figure he made.---The officer made him look in the glass, to try if he could recollect himself, and asked if he was a Capuchin now or not.---He was shocked at his own appearance; but bore every thing with meekness and resignation. They then conducted him to the guard, belabouring him all the way with the cord of St. Francis, and asking him every stroke, if he knew his master now?

In

In the mean time, Pasqual was snug in his convent, enjoying the sweets of his adventure. He had a spare cloak and cowl, and was soon equipped again like one of the holy fathers: he then took the clothes and accoutrements of the lifeguard-man, and laid them in a heap, near the gate of another convent of Capuchins, but at a great distance from his own, reserving only to himself a trifle of money which he found in the breeches pocket, just to indemnify him for the loss of his cloak and his cowl; and even this, he says, he should have held sacred, but he knew whoever should find the clothes, would make lawful prize of it.

The poor soldier remained next day a spectacle of ridicule to all the world; at last his companions heard of his strange metamorphosis, and came in troops to see him: their jokes were perhaps still more galling than those of the guard, but as he thought

thought himself under the finger of God, or at least of St. Januarius, he bore all with meekness and patience; at last his clothes were found, and he was set at liberty; but he believes to this day, that the whole was the work of the devil, sent to chastise him for his sins; and has never since seen his mistress on a Friday, nor passed the statue of St. Januarius without muttering a prayer. Fra Pasqual has told the story to several of his most intimate friends, whom he can depend on, amongst whom is the Abbé T-t-i, who has often had it from his own mouth.

I beg pardon for this long story; had I suspected that it would have run out to half this length, I assure you, I should not have troubled you with it. Perhaps, however, you will think this apology precisely the most unnecessary, and most impertinent part of it all.—This is often the fate of apologies, particularly for long letters;

ters; First, because it always makes them longer;—Secondly,—Hey-day! where are we going now?—To return then to our subject. We had no sooner left the Capuchin convent, than our carriage broke down, long before we reached the city: and as walking (at Palermo as well as Naples) is of all things the most disgraceful, we risked by this unfortunate accident to have our characters blasted for ever. However, Philip, our Sicilian servant, took care to make such a noise about it, that our dignity did not much suffer. He kept a little distance before us, pesting and blasting all the way at their cursed crazy carriages;—and swearing that there never was any thing in the world so infamous: that in a city like Palermo, the capital of all Sicily, Signori of our rank and dignity should be obliged to walk on foot; that it must be an eternal reflection against the place,—and bawled out to every person he met, if there was no coaches

coaches to be had; no carriages of any kind, either for love or money. In fhort, we had not got half through the ftreet, before we had feveral offers from gentlemen of our acquaintance, who lamented exceedingly the indignity we had fuffered, and wondered much, that we did not rather fend forward a fervant for another coach, and wait (in the heat of the fun) till it arrived.

This is not the only time that Philip's wits have been of fervice to us on fuch occafions. A few nights ago, we had a difpute with our coachman; turned him off, and had not provided another. We were unfortunately engaged to go to the great converfation. What was to be done?—No fuch thing as walking.—Should we be caught in the fact, we are difgraced for ever.—It would be worfe than to be caught in that of adultery.—No alternative, however. There was not a coach to be had,

had, and our old coachman would not ferve us for one night only.—Philip made fad wry faces, and fwore the coachman ought to be crucified;—but when he faw us bent on walking, he was ftill more diftreffed; and I really believe, if we had been difcovered, that he would not have ferved us any longer. He therefore fet his wits to work, how he fhould preferve both his mafter's honour and his own place. He at firft hefitated, before he would take up the flambeau; but he would by no means be prevailed on to light it.—" What, " (faid Philip) do you think I have no " more regard for you, than to expofe you " to the eyes of the whole world ? No, no, " Gentlemen; if you will bring yourfelves " to difgrace, you fhall not at leaft make " me the agent of fhewing it: but remem-" ber, if you are obferved walking, no " mortal will believe you keep a coach; " and do you expect after that to be re-" ceived into company ?"—" Well, well, " Philip,

"Philip, do as you pleafe, but we muft go to the converfation."—Philip fhrugged up his fhoulders. — "*Diabolo—che faremo!* "*Andiamo dunque Signori—andiamo.*"— So faying, he led the way, and we followed.

Philip had ftudied the geography of the town; he conducted us through lanes only known to himfelf, and carefully avoided the great ftreet; till at laft we arrived at a little entry, which leads to the converfation rooms; here the carriages ufually ftop. We flipped up the entry in the dark; when Philip, darting into a fhop, lighted his flambeau in an inftant, and came rufhing before us, bawling out,---"*Piazza per gli* "*Signori forreftieri;*"---when all the world immediately made way for us.---After we had got into the rooms, he called fo loud after us, afking at what time he fhould order the coach to return; that, overcome partly by rifibility, and partly by a confcioufnefs sciousness of the deceit; not one of us had power to answer him. Philip, however, followed us, and repeated the question so often, that we were obliged to give him a reply, "*a mezzo notte.*"---At midnight he came to tell us that the coach was ready.—We were curious to see how he would behave on this occasion; for it was not half so difficult to get in unobserved, as to get out: however, Philip's genius was equal to both.—As soon as we got into the entry, he run to the door, bawling out Antonio, as hard as he could roar.—No Antonio answered; and unfortunately, there was a number of gentlemen and ladies going away at the same time. They begged of us, as strangers, to step first into our carriage, and absolutely refused to go out before us. Philip was sadly puzzled.—He first ran up the street, then he ran down, and came back all out of breath, cursing Antonio. "That rascal (said he) is never in the way, and you must turn him off.—

"He

" He pretends that he could not get up his
" coach to the door, for the great crowd of
" carriages; and is waiting about fifty
" yards below.—Voſtri Eccellenzi had better
" ſtep down (ſaid Philip) otherwiſe you
" will be obliged to wait here at leaſt half
" an hour."—We took leave of the company, and ſet off.—Philip ran like a lamp-lighter, till he had almoſt paſſed the carriages, when daſhing his flambeau on the ground, as if by accident, he extinguiſhed it, and getting into a narrow lane, he waited till we came up; when he whiſpered us to follow him,—and conducted us back, by the ſame labyrinth we had come; and thus ſaved us from eternal infamy.—However, he aſſures us, he will not venture it again for his place.

Now, what do you think of a nation where ſuch prejudices as theſe prevail?—It is pretty much the caſe all over Italy.—An Italian nobleman is aſhamed of nothing ſo much

much as making ufe of his legs.—They think their dignity augments by the repofe of their members; and that no man can be truly refpectable, that does not loll away one half of his time on a fofa, or in a carriage.—In fhort, a man is obliged to be indolent and effeminate, not to be defpifed and ridiculous.—What can we expect of fuch a people?—Can they be capable of any thing great or manly, who feem almoft afhamed to appear men!—I own, it furpaffes my comprehenfion; and I blefs my ftars every time that I think of honeft John Bull, even with all his faults.—Will you believe me, that, of all that I have known in Italy, there are fcarce half a dozen that have had fortitude enough to fubdue this moft contemptible of all human prejudices?—The Prince of Campo Franco too in this place, is above it. He is a noble fellow, and both in his perfon and character, greatly refembles our late worthy friend, General Craufurd. He is a major-general too, and
always

always dresses in his uniform, which still increases the resemblance. Every time I see him, he says or does something that recalls strongly to my mind the idea of our noble general.—He laughs at the follies of his country, and holds these wretched prejudices in that contempt they deserve.— " What would the old hardy Romans think " (said he, talking on this subject) were " they permitted to take a view of the oc- " cupations of their progeny?—I should " like to see a Brutus or a Cassius amongst " us for a little;—how the clumsy vulgar " fellows would be hooted.—I dare say " they would soon be glad to return to the " shades again."

Adieu;—for some nights past we have been observing the course of a comet; and as we were the first people here that took notice of it, I assure you, we are looked upon as very profound astronomers. I shall say more of it next letter.—We have now got

got out of our abominable inn, and have taken a final leave of our French landlady. The count Buſhemi, a very amiable young man, has been kind enough to provide us a lodging on the ſea ſhore; one of the cooleſt and moſt agreeable in Palermo.

Ever yours, &c.

LETTER XXVI.

Palermo, July 2d.

OUR comet is now gone; we firſt obſerved it on the 24th. It had no tail, but was ſurrounded with a faintiſh ill defined light, that made it look like a bright ſtar ſhining through a thin cloud. This, in all probability, is owing to an atmoſphere, around the body of the comet, that cauſes a refraction of the rays, and prevents them from reaching us with that diſtinctneſs we obſerve in bodies that have no atmoſphere, —We were ſtill the more perſuaded of this two nights ago, when we had the good fortune to catch the comet juſt paſſing cloſe by a ſmall fixed ſtar, whoſe light was not only conſiderably dimm'd, but we thought we obſerved a ſenſible change of place in the ſtar, as ſoon as its rays fell into the atmosphere of the comet; owing no doubt to the refraction in passing through that atmosphere.—We attempted to trace the line of the comet's course, but as we could find no globe, it was not possible to do it with any degree of precision.—Its direction was almost due north, and its velocity altogether amazing.—We did not observe it so minutely the two or three first nights of its appearance, but on the 30th it was at our zenith here, (latitude 38° 10'; longitude from Lond. 13°) about five minutes after midnight, and last night, the first of July, it passed four degrees to the east of the polar star, nearly at 40 minutes after eight. So that, in less than 24 hours, it has described a great arch in the heavens, upwards of 50 degrees; which gives an idea of the most amazing velocity. Supposing it at the distance of the sun, at this rate of travelling, it would go round the earth's orbit in less than a week. Which makes, I think, considerably more than sixty millions

lions of miles in a day; a motion that vaftly furpaffes all human comprehenfion. And as this motion continues to be greatly accelerated, what muft it be, when the comet approaches ftill nearer to the body of the fun! Laft night a change of place was obfervable in the fpace of a few minutes, particularly when it paffed near any of the fixed ftars. We attempted to find if it had any obfervable parallax, but the vaft rapidity of its motion always prevented us; for whatever fixed ftars it was near in the horizon, it had got fo far to the north of them, long before it reached the meridian, that the parallax, if there was any, entirely efcaped us.

I fhall long much to fee the obfervations that have been made with you, and in other diftant countries, on this comet; as from thefe, we fhall probably be enabled to form fome judgment of its diftance from the earth: which, although we could obferve

no

SICILY AND MALTA.

no parallax, I am apt to believe was not very great, as its motion was so very perceptible.—We could procure no inftruments to meafure its apparent diftance from any of the fixed ftars, fo that the only two obfervations any thing can be made of, are the time of its paffing the polar ftar laft night, its diftance from it, and the time of its arrival at our zenith on the 30th; this we found by applying the eye to a ftraight rod, hung perpendicularly from a fmall thread. The comet was not in the exact point of the zenith, but to the beft of our obfervation, about fix or feven minutes to the north of it. Laft night it was vifible almoft immediately after fun-fet; long before any of the fixed ftars appeared. It is now immerfed in the rays of the fun, and has certainly got very near his body. If it returns again to the regions of fpace, it will probably be vifible in a few days, but I own I fhould much doubt of any fuch return, if it is really by the attractive force

of

of the fun, that it is at prefent carried with fuch amazing celerity towards him. This is the third comet of this kind, whofe return I have had an opportunity of watching; but never was fortunate enough to find any of them after they had paffed the fun; though thofe that do really return, appear at that time much more luminous than before they approached him.

The aftronomy of comets, from what I can remember of it, appears to be clogged with very great difficulties, and even fome feeming abfurdities. It is difficult to conceive, that thefe immenfe bodies, after being drawn to the fun with the velocity of a million of miles in an hour; when they have at laft come almoft to touch him, fhould then fly off from his body, with the fame velocity they approach it; and that too, by the power of this very motion that his attraction has occafioned.—The demonftration of this I remember is very curious

curious and ingenious; but I wish it may be entirely free from sophistry. No doubt, in bodies moving in curves round a fixed center, as the centripetal motion increases, the centrifugal one increases likewise;—— but how this motion, which is only generated by the former, should at last get the better of the power that produces it; and that too, at the very time this power has acquired its utmost force and energy; seems somewhat difficult to conceive. It is the only instance I know, wherein the effect increasing regularly with the cause; at last whilst the cause is still acting with full vigour; the effect entirely gets the better of the cause, and leaves it in the lurch. For, the body attracted, is at last carried away with infinite velocity from the attracting body.—By what power is it carried away?—Why, say our philosophers, by the very power of this attraction, which has now produced a new power superior to itself, to wit, the centrifugal force. How-ever,

ever, perhaps all this may be reconcilable to reaſon; far be it from me to preſume attacking ſo glorious a ſyſtem as that of attraction. The law that the heavenly bodies are ſaid to obſerve, in deſcribing equal areas in equal times, is ſuppoſed to be demonſtrated, and by this it would appear, that the centripetal and centrifugal forces alternately get the maſtery of one another.

However, I cannot help thinking it ſomewhat hard to conceive, that gravity ſhould always get the better of the centrifugal force, at the very time that its action is the ſmalleſt, when the comet is at its greateſt diſtance from the ſun; and that the centrifugal force ſhould get the better of gravity, at the very time that its action is the greateſt, when the comet is at its neareſt point to the ſun.

To a common obſerver it would rather appear, that the ſun, like an electric body,

body, after it had once charged the objects that it attracted with its own effluvia or atmosphere, by degrees loses its attraction, and at last even repels them; and, that the attracting power, like what we likewise observe in electricity, does not return again till the effluvia imbibed from the attracting body is dispelled or dissipated; when it is again attracted, and so on alternately. For it appears (at least to an unphilosophical observer) somewhat repugnant to reason to say that a body flying off from another body some thousands of miles in a minute, should all the time be violently attracted by that body, and that it is even by virtue of this very attraction that it is flying off from it.—He would probably ask, What more could it do, pray, were it really to be repelled?

Had the system of electricity, and of repulsion as well as attraction, been known and established in the last age, I have little doubt

doubt that the profound genius of Newton would have called it to his aid; and perhaps accounted in a more satisfactory manner, for many of the great phænomena of the heavens. To the best of my remembrance, we know of no body that possesses, in any considerable degree, the power of attraction, that in certain circumstances does not likewise possess the power of repulsion.——The magnet, the tourmalin, amber, glass, and every electrical substance. —Now, from analogy, as we find the sun so powerfully endowed with attraction, why may we not likewise suppose him to be possessed of repulsion? Indeed, this very power seems to be confessed by the Newtonians to reside in the sun in a most wonderful degree; for they assure us he repels the rays of light with such amazing force, that they fly upwards of 80 millions of miles in seven minutes. Now why should we confine this repulsion to the rays of light only?—As they are material, may not other

other matter brought near his body, be affected in the fame manner? Indeed one would imagine, that their motion alone would create the moſt violent repulſion; and that the force with which they are perpetually flowing from the fun, would moſt effectually prevent every other body from approaching him; for this we find is the conſtant effect of a rapid ſtream of any other matter.--But let us examine a little more his effects on comets. The tails of theſe bodies, are probably their atmoſpheres rendered highly electrical, either from the violence of their motion, or from their proximity to the fun.—Of all the bodies we know, there is none in fo conſtant and fo violent an electrical ſtate, as the higher regions of our own atmoſphere. Of this I have long been convinced; for, fend up a kite with a ſmall wire about its ſtring, only to the height of 12 or 1300 feet, and at all times it will produce fire, as I have found by frequent experience; ſometimes
when

when the air was perfectly clear, without a cloud in the hemisphere; at other times, when it was thick and hazy, and totally unfit for electrical operations below. Now, as this is the case at so small a height, and as we find the effect still grows stronger, in proportion as the kite advances, (for I have sometimes observed, that a little blast of wind, suddenly raising the kite about a hundred feet, has more than doubled the effect) what must it be in very great elevations?—Indeed we may often judge of it from the violence with which the clouds are agitated, from the meteors formed above the region of the clouds, and particularly from the aurora borealis, which has been observed to have much the same colour and appearance as the matter that forms the tails of comets.

Now what must be the effect of so vast a body as our atmosphere, made strongly electrical, when it happens to approach any other

SICILY AND MALTA.

other body?—It muft always be either violently attracted or repelled, according to the pofitive or negative quality (in the language of electricians) of the body that it approaches.

It has ever been obferved that the tails of comets (juft as we fhould expect, from a very light fluid body, attached to a folid heavy one) are drawn after the comets, as long as they are at a diftance from the fun; but as foon as the comet gets near his body the tail veers about to that fide of the comet that is in the oppofite direction from the fun, and no longer follows the comet, but continues its motion fideways, oppofing its whole length to the medium through which it paffes, rather than allow it in any degree to approach the fun. Indeed, its tendency to follow the body of the comet is ftill obfervable, were it not prevented by fome force fuperior to that tendency; for the tail is always obferved to bend a little to that side from whence the comet is flying. This perhaps is some proof too, that it does not move in an absolute vacuum.

When the comet reaches its perihelion, the tail is generally very much lengthened, perhaps by the rarefaction from the heat; —perhaps by the increase of the sun's repulsion, or that of his atmosphere. It still continues projected, exactly in the opposite direction from the sun; and when the comet moves off again to the regions of space, the tail, instead of following it, as it did on its approach, is projected a vast way before it, and still keeps the body of the comet exactly opposed betwixt it and the sun; till by degrees, as the distance increases, the length of the tail is diminished; the repulsion probably becoming weaker and weaker.

It has likewise been observed, that the length of these tails are commonly in proportion

portion to the proximity of the comet to the fun. That of 1680 threw out a train that would almoft have reached from the fun to the earth. If this had been attracted by the fun, would it not have fallen upon his body? when the comet at that time was not one-fourth of his diameter diftant from him; but inftead of this, it was darted away to the oppofite fide of the heavens, even with a greater velocity than that of the comet itfelf—Now what can this be owing to, if not to a repulfive power in the fun, or his atmofphere?

And, indeed, it would at firft appear but little lefs abfurd, to fay that the tail of the comet is all this time violently attracted by the fun, although it be driven away in an oppofite direction from him, as to fay the fame of the comet itfelf. It is true, this repulfion feems to begin much fooner to affect the tail, than the body of the comet; which is fuppofed always to

pafs

pafs the fun before it begins to fly away from him, which is by no means the cafe with the tail. The repulfive force, therefore, (if there is any fuch) is in a much lefs proportion than the attractive one, and probably juft only enough to counterbalance the latter, when thefe bodies are in their perihelions, and to turn them fo much afide, as to prevent their falling into the body of the fun. The projectile force they have acquired will then carry them out to the heavens, and repulfion probably diminifhing as they recede from the fun's atmofphere, his attraction will again take place and retard their motion regularly, till they arrive at their aphelia, when they once more begin to return to him.

I don't know how you will like all this: —Our comet has led me a dance I very little thought of; and I believe I fhould have done better to fend it at once into the fun, and had done with it: and that, indeed,

indeed, I am apt to believe, will be its fate. For as this comet has no tail, there is, of confequence, no apparent repulfion. If it was repelled, its atmofphere like the others, would be driven away in the oppofite direction from the fun; I therefore do not fee any poffible method it has of efcaping.

Thefe comets are certainly bodies of a very different nature from thofe with tails, to which indeed they appear even to bear a much lefs refemblance than they do to planets: and it is no fmall proof of the little progrefs we have made in the knowledge of the univerfe, that they have not as yet been diftinguifhed by a different name.

This is the third kind of body that has been difcovered in our fyftem, that all appear effentially different from each other, that are probably regulated by different laws,

laws, and intended for very different purpofes.—How much will pofterity be aftonifhed at our ignorance, and wonder that this fyftem fhould have exifted for fo many thoufand years, before we were in the leaft acquainted with one half of it, or had even invented names to diftinguifh its different members!

I have no doubt, that in future ages, the number of the comets, the form of their orbits, and time of their revolutions, will be as clearly demonftrated as that of the planets. It is our countryman, Dr. Halley, who has begun this great work, which may be confidered juft now as in its earlieft infancy.—Thefe bodies, too, with thick atmofpheres, but without tails, will likewife have their proper places afcertained, and will no longer be confounded with bodies to which they bear no refemblance, or connexion.

Comets

Comets with tails have seldom been visible, but on their recess from the sun. It is he that kindles them up, and gives them that alarming appearance in the heavens. —On the contrary, those without tails have seldom, perhaps never, been observed, but on their approach to him. I don't recollect any whose return has been tolerably well ascertained. I remember, indeed, a few years ago, a small one, that was said to have been discovered by a telescope, after it had passed the sun, but never more became visible to the naked eye. This assertion is easily made, and nobody can contradict it; but it does not at all appear probable, that it should have been so much less luminous after it had passed the sun, than before it approached him; and I will own to you, when I have heard that the return of these comets had escaped the eyes of the most acute astronomers, I have been tempted to think, that they did not return at all, but were absorbed in the body of the

the fun, which their violent motion towards him feemed to indicate.—Indeed, I have often wifhed that this difcovery might be made, as it would in fome meafure account for what has as yet been looked upon as unaccountable: that the fun, notwithftanding his daily wafte, from enlightening the univerfe, never appears diminifhed either in fize or light.—Surely this wafte muft be immenfe, and were there not in nature fome hidden provifion for fupplying it, in the fpace of fix thoufand years, fuppofing the world to be no older, the planets muft have got to a much greater diftance from his body, by the vaft diminution of his attraction; they muft likewife have moved much flower, and confequently the length of our year muft have been greatly increafed.—Nothing of all this feems to be the cafe: the diameter of the fun is the fame that ever it was: he neither appears diminifhed, nor our diftance from him increafed: his light, heat,

SICILY AND MALTA.

heat, and attraction seem to be the same as ever; and the motion of the planets round him is performed in the same time; of consequence, his quantity of matter still continues the same.—How then is this vast waste supplied?—May there not be millions of bodies attracted by him, from the boundless regions of space, that are never perceived by us? Comets, on their road to him, have several times been accidentally discovered by telescopes, that were never seen by the naked eye.—Indeed, the number of black spots on the sun seem to indicate that there is always a quantity of matter there, only in a preparation to give light, but not yet refined and pure enough to throw off rays like the rest of his body. For I think we can hardly conceive, that any matter can remain long on the body of the sun without becoming luminous; and so we find these spots often disappear, that is to say, the matter of which they are composed is then perfectly

fectly melted, and has acquired the same degree of heat and light as the rest of his body.—Even in our glafs-houfes, and other very hot furnaces, moſt ſorts of matter very ſoon acquire the ſame colour and appearance as the matter in fuſion, and emit rays of light like it. But how much more muſt this be the caſe at the ſurface of the ſun! when Newton computes, that even at many thouſand miles diſtance from it, a body would acquire a degree of heat two thouſand times greater than that of red hot iron. It has generally been underſtood, that he ſaid the great comet really did acquire this degree of heat; but this is certainly a miſtake: Sir Iſaac's expreſſion, to the beſt of my remembrance, is, that it might have acquired it. And if we conſider the very great ſize of that body, and the ſhort time of its perihelion, the thing will appear impoſſible: nor indeed do I think we can conceive, that a body only as large as our Earth, and the ſpots

on

on the fun are often much larger, could be reduced to fufion, even on his furface, but after a very confiderable fpace of time.

Now, as it feems to be univerfally fuppofed, that the rays of light are really particles of matter, proceeding from the body of the fun, I think it is abfolutely neceffary that we fhould fall upon fome fuch method of fending him back a fupply of thofe rays, otherwife let his ftock be ever fo great, it muft at laft be exhaufted.

I wifh aftronomers would obferve whether the fpots on the fun are not increafed after the appearing of thefe comets; and whether thefe fpots do not difappear again by degrees, like a body that is gradually melted down in a furnace. But there is another confideration too, which naturally occurs: pray what becomes of all this vaft quantity

quantity of matter after it is reduced to light? Is it ever collected again into solid bodies; or is it for ever lost and dissipated, after it has made its journey from the sun to the object it illuminates? It is somewhat strange, that of all that immense quantity of matter poured down on us during the day, that pervades and fills the whole universe; the moment we are deprived of the luminous body, the whole of it, in an instant, seems to be annihilated: —in short, there are a number of difficulties attending the common received doctrine of light; nor do I think there is any point in natural philosophy the solution of which is less satisfactory. If we suppose every ray to be a stream of particles of matter, darting from the luminous body, how can we conceive that these streams may be intersected and pierced by other streams of the same matter ten thousand thousand different ways, without causing the least confusion either to the one or the other?

other? for in a clear night we fee diftinctly any particular ftar that we look at, although the rays coming from that ftar to our eye is pierced for millions of miles before it reaches us, by millions of ftreams of the fame rays, from every other fun and ftar in the univerfe. Now fuppofe, in any other matter that we know of, and one would imagine there ought at leaft to be fome fort of analogy; fuppofe, I fay, we fhould only attempt to make two ftreams pafs one another; water, for inftance, or air, one of the pureft and the moft fluid fubftances we are acquainted with, we find it totally impoffible.—The two ftreams will mutually interrupt and incommode one another, and the ftrongeft will ever carry off the weakeft into its own direction; but if a ftream of light is hit by ten thoufand other ftreams, moving at the rate of ten millions of miles in a minute, it is not even bent by the impreffion, nor in the fmalleft degree diverted from its courfe;

course; but reaches us with the same precision and regularity, as if nothing had interfered with it. Besides, on the supposition that light is real particles of matter moving from the sun to the earth, in the space of seven minutes, how comes it to pass, that with all this wonderful velocity, there seems to be no momentum! for it communicates motion to no body that obstructs its passage, and no body whatever is removed by the percussion.—Supposing we had never heard of this discovery, and were at once to be told of a current of matter flying at the rate of ten millions of miles in a minute, and so large as to cover one half of our globe, would we not imagine that the earth must instantly be torn to pieces by it, or carried off with the most incredible velocity! It will be objected, that the extreme minuteness of the particles of light prevents it from having any such effect;—but as these particles are in such quantity, and so close

to

to each other as to cover the surface of every body that is opposed to them, and entirely to fill up that vast space betwixt the earth and the sun, this objection I should think in a great measure falls to the ground. The particles of air and of water are likewise extremely minute, and a small quantity of these will produce little or no effect, but increase their number, and only give them the millionth part of the velocity that is ascribed to a ray of light, and no force whatever could be able to withstand them.

Adieu.—I have unwarily run myself into the very deeps of philosophy; and find it rather difficult to struggle out again.—I ask your pardon, and promise, if possible, for the future, to steer quite clear of them.—I am sure, whatever this comet may be to the universe, it has been an ignis fatuus to me; for it has led me strangely out of my road, and bewildered me amongst rocks

rocks and quickfands, where I was like to ftick fifty times.

I have forgot whether or not you are a rigid Newtonian; if you are, I believe I had better recant in time, for fear of accidents. I know this is a very tender point; and have feen many of thofe gentlemen, who are good Chriftians too, that can bear with much more temper to hear the divinity of our Saviour called in queftion, than that of Sir Ifaac; and look on a Cartefian or a Ptolomean, as a worfe fpecies of infidel than an atheift.

I remember, when I was at college, to have feen a heretic to their doctrine of gravity, very fuddenly converted by being toffed in a blanket; and another, who denied the law of centripetal and centrifugal forces, foon brought to affent, from having the demonftration made upon his fhoulders, by a ftone whirled at the end of a ftring.

Thefe

These are powerful arguments, and it is difficult to withstand them.—I cry you mercy.—I am without reach of you at present, and you are heartily welcome to wreck your vengeance on my letter.

LETTER XXVII.

Palermo, July 6th.

MANY of the churches here are extremely rich and magnificent. The cathedral (or, as they call it, *Madre Chiefa*) is a venerable Gothic building, and of a large size; it is supported within by eighty columns of Oriental granite, and divided into a great number of chapels, some of which are extremely rich, particularly that of St. Rosolia, the patroness of Palermo, who is held in greater veneration here, than all the persons of the Trinity; and, which is still much more, than even the Virgin Mary herself. The relics of the saint are preserved in a large box of silver, curiously wrought and enriched with precious stones. They perform many miracles, and are looked upon as the greatest treasure of the city. They

They are esteemed a most effectual remedy against the plague, and have often preserved them from that fatal distemper. The saint gained so much credit, in saving them from the last plague of Messina, although it was at two hundred miles distance, that they have, out of gratitude, erected a noble monument to her.—St. Agatha did as much for Catania, but that city has not been so generous to her.— The other riches of this church consist principally in some bones of St. Peter, and a whole arm of St. John the Baptist.— There is likewise a jaw-bone of prodigious efficacy; and some other bones of lesser note.---It contains some things of smaller consequence, which, however, are not altogether without their merit. The monuments of their Norman kings, several of whom lie buried here, are of the finest porphiry, some of them near seven hundred years old, and yet of very tolerable workmanship. Opposite to these, there is a taber-

tabernacle of lapis lazuli. It is about fifteen feet high, and finely ornamented. Some of the presents made to St. Rosolia, are by no means contemptible. A cross of very large brilliants, from the king of Spain, is, I think, the most considerable.

The Sachristie too is very rich: There are some robes embroidered with Oriental pearl, that are near four hundred years old, and yet look as fresh as if done yesterday.

The Jesuits church is equal in magnificence to any thing I have seen in Italy.— The genius of those fathers appears strong in all their works; one is never at a loss to find them out. They have been grossly calumniated; for they certainly had less hypocrisy than any other order of monks.

The

The Chiefa del Pallazzo is entirely encrufted over with ancient mofaic; and the vaulted roof too is all of the fame.—But it is endlefs to talk of churches. Here are upwards of three hundred.—That of Monreale, about five miles diftant from this city, is the next in dignity in the ifland, after the cathedral of Palermo. It is nearly of the fame fize, and the whole is encrufted with mofaic, at an incredible expence. Here are likewife feveral porphiry and marble monuments of the firft kings of Sicily. This cathedral was built by King William the Good, whofe memory is ftill held in great veneration amongft the Sicilians.

The archbifhop of Monreale, is already looked upon as a faint, and indeed he deferves beatification better, I believe, than moft of thofe in the calendar. His income is very great, of which he referves to himfelf juft as much as procures him clothes,

clothes, and the simplest kind of food; all the rest he devotes to charitable, pious, and public uses. He even seems to carry this too far, and denies himself the most common gratifications of life. Such as sleeping on a bed; a piece of luxury he is said never to indulge himself in, but lies every night on straw.—He is, as you may believe, adored by the people, who crowd in his way as he passes, to receive his benediction; which they allege is even of more sovereign efficacy than that of the pope. And indeed so it is, for he never sees an object in distress, but he is sure to relieve him; not trusting alone to the spiritual efficacy of the blessing, but always accompanying it with something solid and temporal: and perhaps this accompaniment is not esteemed the worst part of it. The town and country round Monreale are greatly indebted to his liberality; and in every corner exhibit marks of his munificence. He has just now made a present to

the

the cathedral of a magnificent altar; only about one half of which is finiſhed. It is of maſſive ſilver, exquiſitely wrought, repreſenting in high relief, ſome of the principal ſtories in the Bible, and, I think, will be one of the fineſt in the world.—But what is of much greater utility, he has at his own expence made a noble walk the whole way from this city to Monreale, which was formerly of very difficult acceſs, as it ſtands near the top of a pretty high mountain. The walk is cut with a great deal of judgment on the ſide of this mountain, and winds by eaſy zig-zags to the top of it. It is adorned with ſeveral elegant fountains of water, and is bordered on each ſide with a variety of flowering ſhrubs.— The valley at the foot of the mountain is rich and beautiful. It appears one continued orange garden for many miles, and exhibits an elegant piece of ſcenery; perfuming the air at the ſame time with the moſt delicious odours.—We were ſo pleaſed

with

with this little expedition, that notwithstanding the heat of the feafon, we could not keep in our carriage, but walked almoft the whole of it.

The city of Palermo for thefe ten days paft has been wholly occupied in preparing for the great feaft of St. Rofolia. And if the fhow is in any degree adequate to the expence and trouble it cofts them, it muft indeed be a very noble one. They are erecting an incredible number of arches and pyramids for the illuminations. They are of wood; painted, and adorned with artificial flowers. Thefe, they tell us, are to be entirely covered over with fmall lamps; fo that when feen at a little diftance, they appear like fo many pyramids and arches of flame. The whole Marino, and the two great ftreets that divide the city, are to be illuminated in this magnificent manner. The number of pyramids and arches prepared for thefe illuminations, we are told, exceeds two thousand. They are erected on each side of the street, betwixt the foot path and the pavement, and run in two right lines exactly parallel from end to end. Each of these lines is a mile in length, which makes four miles for the whole. The four gates are the vistas to these four streets, and are to be highly decorated and illuminated. From the square in the centre of the city, the whole of this vast illumination can be seen at once; and they assure us the grandeur of it exceeds all belief.—The whole of the Marino is to be dressed out in the same manner; and for these three weeks past, they have been employed in erecting two great theatres for fireworks. One of these fronts the viceroy's palace, and is almost equal to it in size. The other is laid on piles driven in the sea, exactly opposite to the great orchestra in the centre of the Marino.—— Besides these, they are building an enormous engine, which they call St. Rosolia's

triumphal

triumphal car. From the fize of it, one would imagine it were for ever to remain in the fpot where it is erected; but they affure us, it is to be drawn in triumph through the city. It is indeed mounted upon wheels, but it does not appear that any force whatever can be able to turn them.

I own my curiofity increafes every day to fee the fingular exhibition. The car is already higher than moft houfes in Palermo, and they are ftill adding to its height. But the part of the fhow they value themfelves the moft on, is the illumination of the great church; this they affirm is fuperior to any thing in the world; the illumination of St. Peter's itfelf not excepted. The preparations for it, are indeed amazing. Thefe were begun about a month ago, and will not be finifhed till towards the laft days of the feaft. The whole of the cathedral, both roof and walls,

walls, is entirely covered over with mir-
rour, intermixed with gold and silver
paper, and an infinite variety of artificial
flowers. All thefe are arranged and dif-
pofed, in my opinion, with great tafte and
elegance; none of them predominate, but
they are intermingled every where in a juft
proportion.

Every altar, chapel, and column are
finifhed in the fame manner, which takes
off from the littlenefs of the particular ornaments, and gives an air of grandeur and
uniformity to the whole. The roof is
hung with innumerable luftres filled with
wax candles, and, I am perfuaded, when
the whole is lighted up, it muft be equal to
any palace either in the Fairy Tales or the
Arabian Nights Entertainment. Indeed it
feems pretty much in the fame ftyle too,
for all is gold, filver, and precious ftones.
The faints are dreffed out in all their
glory, and the fairy queen herfelf was
never

never finer than is St. Rosolia.—The people are lying yonder in crowds before her, praying with all their might.—I dare say, for one petition offered to God Almighty, she has at least an hundred.

We were just now remarking, with how little respect they pass the chapels dedicated to God; they hardly deign to give a little inclination of the head; but when they come near those of their favourite saints, they bow down to the very ground: Ignorance and superstition have ever been inseparable:—I believe in their hearts they think he has already reigned long enough; and would be glad to have a change in the government:—and every one of them (like the poor Welchman who thought he should be succeeded by Sir Watkin Williams) is fully persuaded, that his own favourite saint is the true heir apparent. Indeed they already give them the precedency on most occasions; not in processions and affairs

affairs of etiquette; there they think it would not be decent; but in their more private affairs, they generally pay the compliment to the faint:—Yet in their infcriptions on churches and chapels, (which one would think are public enough) when they are dedicated to God and any particular faint, they have often ventured to put the name of the faint firft.—Sancto Januario, et Deo Opt. Max. taking every opportunity of raifing their dignity, though at the expence of that of God himfelf.

LETTER XXVIII.

Palermo, July 7th.

I HAVE been inquiring who this same St. Rosolia may be, who has become so very capital a personage in this part of the world; but, notwithstanding their adoring her with such fervency, I have found none that can give any tolerable account of her saintship. They refer you to the most fabulous legends, that even differ widely in their accounts of her. And, after all the offerings they have made, the churches they have built, and monuments they have raised to her memory, I think it is far from being improbable, that there really never did exist such a person. I went through all the booksellers' shops, but could find nothing relative to her, except an epic poem, of which she is the heroine. It is in the Sicilian language; and is indeed one of the greateſt curioſities I have met with. The poet ſets her at once above all other ſaints except the Virgin, and it ſeems to be with the greateſt reluctance, that he can prevail upon himſelf to yield the pas even to her. I find, from this curious compoſition, and the notes upon it, that St. Roſolia was niece to King William the Good. That ſhe began very early to diſplay ſymptoms of her ſanctity. That at fifteen ſhe deſerted the world, and diſclaimed all human ſociety. She retired to the mountains on the weſt of this city; and was never more heard of for about five hundred years. She diſappeared in the year 1159. The people thought ſhe had been taken up to heaven;- till in the year 1624, during the time of a dreadful plague, a holy man had a viſion, that the ſaint's bones were lying in a cave near the top of the Monte Pelegrino. That if they were taken up with due reverence, and carried in proceſsion thrice round the walls of the city, they should immediately be delivered from the plague. At first little attention was paid to the holy man, and he was looked upon as little better than a dreamer; however, he persisted in his story, grew noisy, and got adherents. The magistrates, to pacify them, sent to the Monte Pelegrino; when lo the mighty discovery was made! —the sacred bones were found,—the city was freed from the plague,—and St. Rosolia became the greatest saint in the calendar.—Churches were reared, altars were dedicated, and ministers appointed to this new divinity, whose dignity and consequence have ever since been supported at an incredible expence. Now I think it is more than probable that these bones, that are now so much reverenced, and about which this great city is at present in such a bustle, belong to some poor wretch that perhaps was murdered, or died for want in the mountains. The holy man probably

could

could have given a very good account of them.

It is really aftonifhing to think, what animals fuperftition makes of mankind.— I dare fay, the bones of St. Rofolia are juft as little entitled to the honours they receive, as thofe of poor *St. Viar*, which were found fomewhere in Spain under a broken tomb-ftone, where thefe were the only legible letters. The ftory I think, is told by Dr. Middleton. The priefts found that the bones had an excellent knack at working miracles, and were of opinion that this, together with the *S. Viar* on the ftone, was proof fufficient of his fanctity. He continued long in high eftimation, and they drew no inconfiderable revenue from his abilities; till unfortunately they petitioned the pope to grant him fome immunities. The pope (Leo the Tenth, I think), not entirely fatisfied with regard to his faintfhip, defired to be informed of his pretenfions.—A lift of his miracles

miracles was sent over, accompanied by the stone with *S. Viar* upon it. The first part of the proof was sustained; but the antiquaries discovered the fragment to be part of the tomb-stone of a (Roman) *præfectus viarum,* or overseer of the high roads; to whose bones they had been so much indebted; and poor St. Viar, though probably an honester man than most of them, was ordered to be struck out of the calendar.

The people of fashion here hold the superstition of the vulgar in great contempt; and perhaps that very superstition is one principal cause of their infidelity. Indeed I have ever found, that deism is most prevalent in those countries where the people are the wildest and most bigotted.—A refined and cultivated understanding, shocked at their folly, thinks it cannot possibly recede too far from it, and is often tempted to fly to the very opposite extreme.—When reason is much offended by any particular dogma of faith

faith or act of worship, she is but too apt, in the midst of her disgust, to reject the whole. The great misfortune is, that, in these countries, the most violent champions for religion are commonly the most weak and ignorant: —And certainly, one weak advocate in any cause, but more particularly in a mysterious one, that requires to be handled with delicacy and address, is capable of hurting it more, than fifty of its warmest opponents.—Silly books, that have been written by weak well-meaning men, in defence of religion, I am confident have made more infidels than all the works of Bolingbroke, Shaftesbury, or even Voltaire himself: they only want to make people believe that there are some ludicrous things to be said against it; but these grave plodding blockheads do all they can to persuade us that there is little thing to be said for it. —The universal error of these gentry, is that they ever attempt to explain, and reconcile to sense and reason, those very mysteries

teries that the first principles of our religion teach us are incomprehensible; and of consequence neither objects of sense nor reason.—I once heard an ignorant priest declare, that he did not find the least difficulty, in conceiving the mystery of the Trinity, or that of incarnation; and that he would undertake to make them plain to the meanest capacities. A gentleman present told him, he had no doubt he could, to all such capacities as his own. The priest took it as a compliment, and made him a bow.—Now don't you think, that a few such teachers as this, must hurt religion more by their zeal, than all its opponents can by their wit? Had these heroes still kept behind the bulwarks of faith and of mystery, their adversaries never could have touched them; but they have been foolish enough to abandon these strong holds, and dared them forth to combat on the plain fields of reason and of sense.—A sad piece of generalship indeed: such defenders must ever ruin the best cause.

But

But although the people of education here defpife the wild fuperftition of the vulgar, yet they go regularly to mafs, and attend the ordinances with great refpect and decency; and they are much pleafed with us for our conformity to their cuftoms, and for not appearing openly to defpife their rites and ceremonies. I own, this attention of theirs, not to offend weak minds, tends much to give us a favourable opinion both of their hearts and underftandings. They don't make any boaft of their infidelity; neither do they pefter you with it as in France, where it is perpetually buzz'd in your ears; and where, although they pretend to believe lefs, they do in fact believe more than any nation on the continent.

I know of nothing that gives one a worfe opinion of a man, than to fee him make a fhow and parade of his contempt for things held facred: it is an open infult to the
judgment

judgment of the public. A countryman of ours, about two years ago, offended egregiously in this article, and the people still speak of him both with contempt and detestation. It happened one day, in the great church, during the elevation of the host, when every body else were on their knees, that he still kept standing, without any appearance of respect to the ceremony. A young nobleman that was near him expressed his surprise at this. "It is strange, "Sir, (said he) that you, who have had "the education of a gentleman, and ought "to have the sentiments of one, should "chuse thus to give so very public offence." "Why, Sir, (said the Englishman) I don't "believe in transubstantiation."—"Neither "do I, Sir, (replied the other) and yet you "see I kneel."

Adieu. I am called away to see the preparations for the feast. In my next I shall probably give you some account of it.

P. S. I have been watching with great care the return of our comet, but as yet I have difcovered nothing of it: I obferve too, with a very indifferent glafs, feveral large round fpots on the fun's difk, and am far from being certain that it is not one of them : but I fhall not alarm you any more with this fubject.

LETTER XXIX.

Palermo, July 10th.

ON Sunday, the 8th, we had the long expected Sirocc wind, which, although our expectations had been raised pretty high, yet I own it greatly exceeded them. Ever since we came to our new lodging, the thermometer has stood betwixt 72 and 74; at our old one, it was often at 79 and 80; so great is the difference betwixt the heart of the city and the sea-shore. At present, our windows not only front to the North, but the sea is immediately under them, from whence we are constantly refreshed by a delightful cooling breeze. Friday and Saturday were uncommonly cool, the mercury never being higher than $72\frac{1}{2}$; and although the Sirocc is said to have set in early on Sunday morning, the air in our apart-

apartments, which are very large, with high cielings, was not in the leaſt affected by it at eight o'clock, when I roſe.—I opened the door without having any ſuſpicion of ſuch a change; and indeed I never was more aſtoniſhed in my life.—The firſt blaſt of it on my face felt like the burning ſteam from the mouth of an oven. I drew back my head and ſhut the door, calling out to Fullarton, that the whole atmoſphere was in a flame. However, we ventured to open another door that leads to a cool platform, where we uſually walk; this was not expoſed to the wind; and here I found the heat much more ſupportable than I could have expected from the firſt ſpecimen I had of it at the other door. It felt ſomewhat like the ſubterraneous ſweating ſtoves at Naples; but ſtill much hotter.—In a few minutes we found every fibre greatly relaxed, and the pores opened to ſuch a degree, that we expected ſoon to be thrown into a profuſe ſweat. I went to examine the

the thermometer, and found the air in the room as yet so little affected, that it stood only at 73. The preceding night it was at 72¼. I took it out to the open air, when it immediately rose to 110, and soon after to 112; and I am confident, that in our old lodgings, or any where within the city, it must have risen several degrees higher. The air was thick and heavy, but the barometer was little affected; it had fallen only about a line. The sun did not once appear the whole day, otherwise I am persuaded the heat must have been insupportable; on that side of our platform which is exposed to the wind, it was with difficulty we could bear it for a few minutes. Here I exposed a little pomatum which was melted down, as if I had laid it before the fire. I attempted to take a walk in the street, to see if any creature was stirring, but I found it too much for me, and was glad to get up stairs again.

This

This extraordinary heat continued till 3 o'clock in the afternoon, when the wind changed at once, almoſt to the oppoſite point of the compaſs, and all the reſt of the day it blew ſtrong from the ſea. It is impoſſible to conceive the different feeling of the air. Indeed, the ſudden change from heat to cold is almoſt as inconceivable as that from cold to heat. The current of this hot air had been flying for many hours from South to North; and I had no doubt, that the atmoſphere, for many miles round, was entirely compoſed of it; however, the wind no ſooner changed to the North, than it felt extremely cold, and we were ſoon obliged to put on our clothes, for till then we had been almoſt naked. In a ſhort time the thermometer ſunk to 82, a degree of heat that in England would be thought almoſt inſupportable, and yet all that night we were obliged, merely from the cold, to keep up the glaſſes of our coach; ſo much were the pores opened and the fibres relaxed by these few hours of the Sirocc. Indeed, I had exposed myself a good deal to the open air, as I was determined to feel what effect it would produce on the human body. At first I thought it must have been impossible to bear it; but I soon discovered my mistake, and found, that where I was sheltered from the wind, I could walk about without any great inconveniency; neither did it produce that copious sweat I expected; it occasioned indeed a violent perspiration, which was only attended with a slight moisture on the skin; but I suppose, if I had put on my clothes, or taken the least exercise, it soon would have brought it on.

I own to you my curiosity with regard to the Sirocc is now thoroughly satisfied; nor do I at all wish for another visit of it during our stay in Sicily. Many of our acquaintance who had been promising us this *regalo*, as they call it, came crowding about

about us as foon as it was over, to know what we thought of it. They own it has been pretty violent for the time it lafted; but affure us they have felt it more fo, and likewife of a much longer duration; however, it feldom lafts more than thirty-fix or forty hours, fo that the walls of the houfes have not time to be heated throughout, otherwife they think there could be no fuch thing as living; however, from what I felt of it, I believe they are miftaken. Indeed, had I been fatisfied with the firft blaft, (which is generally the cafe with them) and never more ventured out in it, I certainly fhould have been of their opinion. They laughed at us for expofing ourfelves fo long to it; and were furprifed that our curiofity fhould lead us to make experiments at the expence of our perfons. They affure us, that during the time it lafts, there is not a mortal to be feen without doors, but thofe whom neceffity obliges. All their doors and windows are fhut clofe, to prevent the external air from entering; and where there are no window-shutters, they hang up wet blankets on the inside of the window. The servants are constantly employed in sprinkling water, through their apartments, to preserve the air in as temperate a state as possible; and this is no difficult matter here, as I am told there is not a house in the city that has not a fountain within it. By these means the people of fashion suffer very little from the Sirocc, except the strict confinement to which it obliges them.

It is somewhat singular, that notwithstanding the scorching heat of this wind, it has never been known to produce any epidemical distempers, nor indeed bad consequences of any kind to the health of the people. It is true, they feel extremely weak and relaxed during the time it blows, but a few hours of the Tramontane, or North wind, which generally succeeds it, soon
braces

braces them up, and fets them to rights again. Now, in Naples, and in many other places in Italy, where its violence is not to be compared to this, it is often attended with putrid diforders, and feldom fails to produce almoſt a general dejection of fpirits. It is true, indeed, that there the Sirocc lafts for many days; nay, even for weeks; fo that, as its effects are different, it probably proceeds likewife from a different caufe.

I have not been able to procure any good account of this very fingular object in the climate of Palermo. The caufes they affign for it are various, though none of them, I think, altogether fatisfactory.

I have feen an old fellow here, who has written upon it. He fays, it is the fame wind that is fo dreadful in the fandy defarts of Africa, where it fometimes proves mortal in the fpace of half an hour. He alleges that

that it is cooled by its paſſage over the ſea, which entirely diſarms it of theſe tremendous effects, before it reaches Sicily. But if this were true, we ſhould expect to find it moſt violent on that ſide of the iſland that lies neareſt to Africa, which is not the caſe:—though indeed it is poſſible that its heat may be again increaſed by its paſſage acroſs the iſland; for it has ever been found much more violent at Palermo, which is near the moſt northern point, than any where elſe in Sicily.—Indeed, I begin to be more reconciled to this reaſon, when I conſider that this city is almoſt ſurrounded by high mountains, the ravines and vallies betwixt which are parched up and burning hot at this ſeaſon. Theſe likewiſe contain innumerable ſprings of warm water, the ſtreams of which muſt tend greatly to increaſe the heat, and perhaps likewiſe to ſoften the air, and diſarm it of its noxious qualities. It is a practice too, at this ſeaſon, to burn heath and bruſhwood on the mountains,

tains, which muſt ſtill add to the heat of the air.

Some gentlemen who were in the country told me, that they walked out immediately after the Sirocc, and found the graſs and plants, that had been green the day before, were become quite brown, and crackled under their feet as if dried in an oven.

I ſhall add for your amuſement, a journal of the weather ſince we came to Palermo. The barometer has continued conſtantly within a line or two of the ſame point, $29\frac{1}{2}$;—and the ſky has been always clear, except the day of the Sirocc and the 26th of June, when we had a pretty ſmart ſhower of rain for two hours; ſo that I think I have nothing farther to do, but to mark the heights of the thermometer.

	Thermometer.
June 17	$73\frac{1}{2}$
18	74

June

					Thermometer.
June	19	-	-	-	75
	20	-	-	-	76
	21	-	-	-	$75\frac{1}{2}$
	22	-	-	-	77
	23	-	-	-	$76\frac{1}{2}$
	24	-	-	-	77
	25	-	-	-	77
	26	-	-	-	$77\frac{1}{2}$
	27	-	-	-	77
	28	-	-	-	$77\frac{1}{2}$
	29	-	-	-	$77\frac{1}{2}$
	30	-	-	-	$78\frac{1}{2}$
July	1	-	-	-	79
	2	-	-	-	80
	3	-	-	-	$80\frac{1}{2}$
	4	At our new lodgings on the sea-side fronting the North,			74
	5	-	-	-	73
	6	-	-	-	$72\frac{1}{2}$
	7	-	-	-	$72\frac{1}{2}$
	8	The Sirocc wind,	-		112
		In the afternoon,	-		82
	9	-	-	-	79
	10	-	-	-	78

The

SICILY AND MALTA.

The more I confider the extreme violence of this heat, the more I am furprifed that we were able to bear it with fo little inconvenience. We did not even feel that depreffion of fpirits that commonly attends very great heats with us.—The thermometer rofe 40 degrees, or very near it; and it happens fingularly enough, that before the Sirocc began, it ftood juft about 40 degrees above the point of congelation; fo that in the morning of the 8th of July, the heat increafed as much, almoft inftantaneoufly, as it generally does during the whole time that the fun moves from tropic to tropic; for the difference of 72 and 112 is the fame as between the freezing point and 72; or between a cold day in winter, and a warm one in fummer.

Yefterday we had a great entertainment in the palace of the Prince Partana, from the balcony of which the viceroy reviewed a regiment of Swifs, the beft I have yet feen seen in the Neapolitan service. They are really a fine body of men, and, notwithstanding the violence of the heat, went through their motions with great spirit. They had two field-pieces on each flank, which were extremely well served; and the evolutions were performed with more precision and steadiness than one generally meets with, except in England or Germany. The grenadiers were furnished with false grenades, which produced every effect of real ones, except that of doing mischief. The throwing of these was the part of the entertainment that seemed to please the most; and the grenadiers took care to direct them so, that their effect should not be lost. When a number of them fell together amongst a thick crowd of the mobility, which was commonly the case, it afforded an entertaining scene enough, for they defended themselves with their hats, and threw them very dexterously upon their neighbours. However, we saw no damage

mage done, except the fingeing of a few wigs and caps; for the ladies were there in as great numbers as the gentlemen.

The company at the Prince Partana's was brilliant, and the entertainment noble. It confifted principally of ices, creams, chocolate, fweet-meats, and fruit, of which there was a great variety. Not one half of the company play'd at cards; the reft amufed themfelves in converfation and walking on the terras. We found the young prince and princefs, who are very amiable, with feveral of their companions, playing at crofs-purpofes, and other games of that kind. We were joyfully admitted of this cheerful little circle, where we amufed ourfelves very well for feveral hours.—I only mention this, to fhew you the different fyftem of behaviour here and in Italy, where no fuch familiar intercourfe is allowed amongft young people before marriage. The young ladies here are eafy, affable,

affable, and unaffected; and not (as on the continent) perpetually stuck up by the sides of their mothers, who bring them into company, not for their amusement, but rather to offer them to sale; and seem mightily afraid lest every one should steal them, or that they themselves should make an elopement; which indeed I should think there was some danger of, considering the restraint under which they are kept:—for surely there is no such strong incitement to vice, as the making a punishment of virtue.

Here the mothers shew a proper confidence in their daughters, and allow their real characters to form and to ripen. In the other case they have either no character at all, or an affected one, which they take care to throw off the moment they have got a husband; when they think it impossible to recede too far from those rigorous maxims of decorum and circumspection, the

practice

practice of which they had ever found fo extremely difagreeable.

Were they allowed firft to fhew what they really are, I am perfuaded they would not be half fo bad; but their parents, by the manner they treat them, fhew that they have no confidence in their principles; and feem to have adopted the ungenerous maxim of our countryman,

"That every woman is at heart a rake."

Now in countries where this maxim becomes of general belief, there is no doubt, that it likewife becomes true; for the women having no longer any character to fupport, they will even avoid the pretences to virtue, well knowing that thofe pretences are only looked upon as hypocrify and affectation. I dare fay, you will agree with me, that the better method to make them virtuous, is firft to make them believe that we think them fo; for where virtue is really efteemed, esteemed, there are none that would willingly relinquish the character; but where it requires a guard, (as parson Adams says) it certainly is not worth the centinel.

Some of the families here put me in mind of our own domestic system. The prince of Resuttana, his wife and daughter, are always together; but it is because they chuse to be so, and there appears the strongest affection, without the least diffidence on the one side, or restraint on the other.—The young princess Donna Rosolia is one of the most amiable young ladies I have seen; she was of our little party last night, and indeed made one of its greatest ornaments. —It would appear vain and partial, after this to say, that in countenance, sentiment, and behaviour, she seems altogether English;—but it is true:—and this perhaps may have contributed to advance her still higher in our esteem; for in spite of all our philosophy, these unphilosophical prejudices

judices will still exist, and no man, I believe, has entirely divested himself of them. —We had lately a noble entertainment at her father's country-house, and had reason to be much pleased with the unaffected hospitality and easy politeness of the whole family. This palace is reckoned the most magnificent in the neighbourhood of Palermo. It lies about six or seven miles to the west of the city, in the country called Il Colle; in the opposite direction from the Bagaria, which I have already mentioned. The viceroy and his family, with the greatest part of the nobility, were of this party, which lasted till about two in the morning. At midnight a curious set of fire-works were played off, from the leads of the palace, which had a fine effect from the garden below.

Farewell.—I had no time to write yesterday, and though we did not break up till near three this morning, I have got up

at

at eight, I was so eager to give you some account of the Siroco wind.

We are now going to be very busy: The feast of St. Rosolia begins to-morrow; and all the world are on the very tip-toe of expectation: perhaps they may be disappointed. I often wish that you were with us, particularly when we are happy: Though you know it is by no means feasts and shows that make us so. However, as this is perhaps the most remarkable one in Europe; that you may enjoy as much of it as possible, I shall sit down every night, and give you a short account of the transactions of the day.—We are now going to breakfast; after which we are engaged to play at Ballon, an exercise I suppose you are well acquainted with; but as the day promises to be extremely hot, I believe I shall desert the party and go a swimming.—But I see F. and G. have already attacked the figs and peaches, so I must appear for my interest.— Farewell.

LETTER XXX.

Palermo, July 12th.

ABOUT five in the afternoon, the feſtival began by the triumph of St. Roſolia, who was drawn with great pomp through the centre of the city, from the Marino to the Porto Nuovo. The triumphal car was preceded by a troop of horſe, with trumpets and kettle-drums; and all the city officers in their gala uniforms. It is indeed a moſt enormous machine: It meaſures ſeventy feet long, thirty wide, and upwards of eighty high; and, as it paſſed along, over-topped the loftieſt houſes of Palermo. The form of its underpart is like that of the Roman gallies, but it ſwells as it advances in height; and the front aſſumes an oval ſhape like an amphitheatre,

theatre, with seats placed in the theatrical manner. This is the great orchestra, which was filled with a numerous band of musicians placed in rows, one above the other: Over this orchestra and a little behind it, there is a large dome supported by six Corinthian columns, and adorned with a number of figures of saints and angels; and on the summit of the dome there is a gigantic silver statue of St. Rosolia.—The whole machine is dressed out with orange-trees, flower-pots, and trees of artificial coral. The car stopped every fifty or sixty yards, when the orchestra performed a piece of music, with songs in honour of the saint. It appeared a moving castle, and completely filled the great street from side to side. This indeed was its greatest disadvantage, for the space it had to move in was in no wise proportioned to its size, and the houses seemed to dwindle away to nothing as it passed along. This vast fabric was drawn by fifty-six huge mules,

SICILY AND MALTA.

mules, in two rows, curiously caparisoned, and mounted by twenty-eight postilions, dressed in gold and silver stuffs, with great plumes of ostrich feathers in their hats.— Every window and balcony, on both sides of the street, were full of well-dressed people, and the car was followed by many thousands of the lower sort. The triumph was finished in about three hours; and was succeeded by the beautiful illumination of the Marino.

I believe I have already mentioned, that there is a range of arches and pyramids extending from end to end of this noble walk: these are painted, and adorned with artificial flowers, and are entirely covered with lamps, placed so very thick, that at a little distance the whole appears so many pyramids and arches of flame. The whole chain of this illumination was about a mile in length, and indeed you can hardly conceive any thing more splendid. There was no break or imperfection any where; the night being so still that not a single lamp was extinguished.

Opposite to the centre of this great line of light, there was a magnificent pavilion erected for the viceroy and his company, which consisted of the whole nobility of Palermo: and on the front of this, at some little distance in the sea, stood the great fire-works, representing the front of a palace, adorned with columns, arches, trophies, and every ornament of architecture. All the chebecks, galleys, galliots, and other shipping, were ranged around this palace, and formed a kind of amphitheatre in the sea, inclosing it in the centre.—These began the show by a discharge of the whole of their artillery, the sound of which, re-echoed from the mountains, produced a very noble effect; they then played off a variety of water rockets, and bombs of a curious construction, that often

often burſt below water. This continued for half an hour, when in an inſtant, the whole of the palace was beautifully illuminated. This was the ſignal for the ſhipping to ceaſe, and appeared indeed like a piece of enchantment, as it was done altogether inſtantaneouſly, and without the appearance of any agent. At the ſame time the fountains that were repreſented in the court before the palace, began to ſpout up fire, and made a repreſentation of ſome of the great *jet d'eaus* of Verſailles and Marly. As ſoon as theſe were extinguiſhed, the court aſſumed the form of a great parterre; adorned with a variety of palm-trees of fire, interſperſed with orange-trees, flower-pots, vaſes and other ornaments. On the extinguiſhing of theſe the illumination of the palace was likewiſe extinguiſhed; and the front of it broke out into the appearance of a variety of ſuns, ſtars, and wheels of fire, which in a ſhort time reduced it to a perfect ruin.

And when all appeared finiſhed, there burſt from the centre of the pile, a vaſt exploſion of two thouſand rockets, bombs, ſerpents, ſquibs, and devils, which ſeemed to fill the whole atmoſphere: the fall of theſe made terrible havoc amongſt the clothes of the poor people who were not under cover, but afforded admirable entertainment to the nobility who were. During this exhibition we had a handſome entertainment of coffee, ices, and ſweetmeats, with a variety of excellent wines, in the great pavilion in the centre of the Marino; this was at the expence of the Duke of Caſtellano, the prætor (or mayor) of the city. The principal nobility give theſe entertainments by turns every night during the feſtival, and vie with each other in their magnificence,

As ſoon as the fireworks were finiſhed, the viceroy went out to ſea in a galley richly illuminated. We choſe to ſtay on ſhore,

shore, to see the appearance it made at a distance. It was rowed by seventy-two oars, and indeed made one of the most beautiful objects you can imagine; flying with vast velocity over the waters, as smooth and as clear as glass, which shone round it like a flame, and reflected its splendour on all sides. The oars beat time to the French-horns, clarionets, and trumpets, of which there was a numerous band on the prow.

The day's entertainment was concluded by the Corso, which began exactly at midnight, and lasted till two in the morning.

The great street was illuminated in the same magnificent manner as the Marino. The arches and pyramids were erected at little distances from each other, on both sides of the street, betwixt the foot-path and the space for carriages; and when seen from either of the gates, appeared to be two continued lines of the brighteſt flame. Indeed, theſe illuminations are ſo very different, and ſo much ſuperior, to any I have ever ſeen, that I find it difficult to give any tolerable idea of them.—Two lines of coaches occupied the ſpace betwixt theſe two lines of illumination. They were in the greateſt gala; and as they open from the middle, and let down on each ſide, the beauty of the ladies, the richneſs of their dreſs, and brilliance of their jewels, were diſplayed in the moſt advantageous manner.

This beautiful train moved ſlowly round and round for the ſpace of two hours; and every member of it ſeemed animated with a deſire to pleaſe.—The company appeared all joy and exultation:—Scarce two coaches paſſed without ſome mutual acknowledgment of affection or reſpect; and the pleaſure that ſparkled from every eye ſeemed to be reflected and communicated by by a kind of sympathy through the whole.

In such an assembly, it was impossible for the heart not to dilate and expand itself;—I own mine was often so full, that I could hardly find utterance; and I have seen a tragedy with less emotion than I did this scene of joy.—I always thought these affections had been strangers to pomp and parade; but here the universal joy seemed really to spring from the heart: it brightened up every countenance, and spoke affection and friendship from every face.—No stately air,—no supercilious look;—all appeared friends and equals.—And sure I am, that the beauty of the ladies was not half so much heightened either by their dress or their jewels, as by that air of complacency and good humour with which it was animated.

We

We were diftributed in different coaches amongft the nobility, which gave us a better opportunity of making thefe obfervations.—I will own to you, that I have never beheld a more delightful fight:— and if fuperftition often produces fuch effects, I fincerely wifh we had a little more of it amongft us. I could have thrown myfelf down before St. Rofolia, and bleffed her for making fo many people happy.

We retired about two o'clock; but the variety of glittering fcenes and gaudy objects ftill vibrated before my eyes, and prevented me from fleeping; however, I am almoft as much refrefhed as if I had: but I really believe four more fuch days will be too much for any of us. Indeed, I am fure that it is impoffible to keep it up, and it muft neceffarily flag. I think, from what I can obferve, they have already exhaufted almoft one half of their preparations;

rations; how they are to support the other four days, I own, I do not comprehend;—however, we shall see.

I thought to have given you an account of every thing at night, after it was over, but I find it impossible: the spirits are too much dissipated, and exhausted, and the imagination is too full of objects to be able to separate them with any degree of regularity.—I shall write you therefore regularly the morning following, when this fever of the fancy has had time to cool, and when things appear as they really are.—Adieu then till to-morrow.—Here is a fine shower, which will cool the air, and save the trouble of watering the Marino and the great street, which is done regularly every morning when there is no rain. The thermometer is at 73.

13th. I thought there would be a falling off.—Yesterday's entertainments were not so splendid as those of the day before. They began by the horse-races. There were three races, and six horses started each race. These were mounted by boys of about twelve years old, without either saddle or bridle, but only a small piece of cord, by way of bit, in the horse's mouth, which it seems is sufficient to stop them. The great street was the course; and to this end it was covered with earth to the depth of five or six inches.—The firing of a cannon at the Porto Felice was the signal for starting: and the horses seemed to understand this, for they all set off at once, full speed, and continued at their utmost stretch to the Porto Nuovo, which was the winning post. It is exactly a mile, and they performed it in a minute and thirty-five seconds, which, considering the size of the horses, (scarce fourteen hands) we thought was very great. These are generally Barbs, or a mixed breed betwixt the Sicilian and Barb. The boys were gaudily dressed, dreffed, and made a pretty appearance.— We were furprifed to fee how well they ftuck on; but indeed, I obferved they had generally laid faft hold of the mane.

The moment before ftarting, the ftreet appeared full of people; nor did we conceive how the race could poffibly be performed. Our furprife was increafed when we faw the horfes run full fpeed at the very thickeft of this crowd, which did not begin to open, till they were almoft clofe upon it.—The people then opened, and fell back on each fide, by a regular uniform motion, from one end of the ftreet to the other. This fingular manœuvre feemed to be performed without any buftle or confufion, and the moment the horfes were paft, they clofed again behind them. However, it deftroys great part of the pleafure of the race; for you cannot help being under apprehenfions for fuch a number of people, whom you every moment fee

in

in imminent danger of being trod to death; for this must inevitably be their fate, were they only a second or two later in retiring. These accidents, they allow, have often happened; however, yesterday every body escaped.

The victor was conducted along the street in triumph, with his prize displayed before him. This was a piece of white silk embroidered and worked with gold.

These races I think are much superior to the common style of races in Italy, which are performed by horses alone without riders; but they are by no means to be compared to those in England.

The great street was illuminated in the same manner as on the preceding night; and the grand conversation of the nobles was held at the archbishop's palace, which was richly fitted up for the occasion.

The

The gardens were finely illuminated; and put me in mind of our Vauxhall. There were two orcheſtras (one at each end) and two very good bands of muſic. The entertainment was ſplendid, and the archbiſhop ſhewed attention and politeneſs to every perſon of the company.

About ten o'clock the great triumphal car marched back again in proceſſion to the Marino. It was richly illuminated with large wax tapers, and made a moſt formidable figure.—Don Quixote would have been very excuſable in taking it for an inchanted caſtle, moving through the air.— We did not leave the archbiſhop's till midnight, when the Corſo began, which was preciſely the ſame in every reſpect as the night before, and afforded us a delightful ſcene.

14th. Laſt night the two great ſtreets and the four gates of the city that terminate

minate them, were illuminated in the moſt ſplendid manner.—Theſe ſtreets croſs each other in the centre of the city, where they form a beautiful ſquare, called *La Piazza Ottangolare*, from the eight angles they form. This ſquare was richly ornamented with tapeſtry, ſtatues, and artificial flowers; and as the buildings which form its four ſides are uniform, and of a beautiful architecture, and at the ſame time highly illuminated, it made a fine appearance. There are four orcheſtras erected in it: and the four bands of muſic are greater than I had any conception this city could have produced.

From the centre of this ſquare you have a view of the whole city of Palermo thus dreſſed out in its glory; and indeed, the effect it produces ſurpaſſes belief. The four gates that form the viſtas to this ſplendid ſcene are highly decorated, and lighted up in an elegant taſte; the illuminations

minations reprefenting a variety of trophies, the arms of Spain, thofe of Naples, Sicily, and the city of Palermo, with their guardian geniufes, &c.

The converfation of the nobles was held in the viceroy's palace; and the entertainment was ftill more magnificent than any of the former. The great fireworks oppofite to the front of the palace began at ten o'clock, and ended at midnight; after which we went to the Corfo, which lafted, as ufual, till two in the morning. This part of the entertainment ftill pleafes us the moft; it is indeed the only part of it that reaches the heart; and where this is not the cafe, a puppet-fhow is juft as good as a coronation.—We have now got acquainted almoft with every countenance; and from that air of goodnefs and benignity that animates them, and which feems to be mutually reflected from one to the other, we are inclined to form the moſt favourable opinion of the people.

Our fireworks laſt night were greater than thoſe of the Marino, but their effect did not pleaſe me ſo much; the want of the ſea and the ſhipping were two capital wants. They likewiſe repreſented the front of a palace, but of a greater extent. It was illuminated too as the former, and the whole conducted pretty much in the ſame manner. We ſaw it to the greateſt advantage from the balconies of the ſtate apartments, in the viceroy's palace, where we had an elegant concert; but, to the no ſmall diſappointment of the company, Gabrieli, the fineſt ſinger, but the moſt capricious mortal upon earth, did not chuſe to perform.

15th. Three races, ſix horſes each, as formerly. They called it very good ſport. I cannot ſay that I admired it.—A poor creature

creature was rode down, and I believe killed; and one of the boys had likewife a fall.

The great affembly of the nobility was held at the Judice Monarchia's, an officer of high truft and dignity. Here we had an entertainment in the fame ftyle as the others, and a good concert.—At eleven o'clock the viceroy, attended by the whole company, went on foot to vifit the fquare and the great church.—We made a prodigious train; for though the city was all a lamp of light, the fervants of the viceroy and nobility attended with wax flambeaux, to fhew us the way. As foon as the viceroy entered the fquare, the four orcheftras ftruck up a fymphony, and continued playing till he left it.

The crowd around the church was very great, and without the prefence of the viceroy, it would have been impoffible for us to get in: but his attendants foon cleared the paffages; and at once entering the great gate, we beheld the moft fplendid fcene in the world. The whole church appeared a flame of light; which, reflected from ten thoufand bright and fhining furfaces, of different colours and at different angles, produced an effect, which, I think, exceeds all the defcriptions of enchantment I have ever read. Indeed, I did not think that human art could have devifed any thing fo fplendid. I believe I have already mentioned that the whole church, walls, roof, pillars, and pilafters were entirely covered over with mirror, interfperfed with gold and filver paper, artificial flowers, &c. done up with great tafte and elegance, fo that not one inch either of ftone or plaifter was to be feen.—Now, form an idea, if you can, of one of our great cathedrals dreffed out in this manner, and illuminated with twenty thoufand wax tapers, and you will have fome faint notion

of

of this splendid scene.—I own it did greatly exceed my expectations, although, from the descriptions we had of it, they were raised very high.—When we recovered from our first surprise, which had produced, unknown to ourselves, many exclamations of astonishment, I observed that all the eyes of the nobility were fixed upon us; and that they enjoyed exceedingly the amazement into which we were thrown.—Indeed this scene, in my opinion, greatly exceeds all the rest of the show.

I have often heard the illumination of St. Peter's spoken of as a wonderful fine thing: so indeed it is; but it is certainly no more to be compared to this, than the planet Venus is to the sun.—The effects indeed are of a different kind, and cannot well be compared together.

This scene was too glaring to bear any considerable time; and the heat occasioned by the immenfe number of lights, foon became intolerable.—I attempted to reckon the number of luftres, and counted upwards of five hundred; but my head became giddy, and I was obliged to give it up.—They affure us that the number of wax tapers is not lefs than twenty thoufand. There are eight-and-twenty altars, fourteen on each fide; thefe are dreffed out with the utmoft magnificence; and the great altar is ftill the moft fplendid of all.

When you think of the gaudy materials that compofe the lining of this church; it will be difficult to annex an idea of grandeur and majefty to it: at leaft, fo it ftruck me, when I was firft told of it; yet, I affure you, the elegant fimplicity and unity of the defign prevents this effect, and gives an air of dignity to the whole.

It

It is on this part of the show the people of Palermo value themselves the most; they talk of all the rest as trifling in comparison of this; and indeed, I think it is probable, that there is nothing of the kind in the world that is equal to it.—It is strange they should chuse to be at so great an expence and trouble, for a show of a few hours only; for they have already begun this morning, to strip the church of its gaudy dress, and I am told it will not be finished for many weeks.

From the church we went immediately to the Corso, which concluded, as usual, the entertainments of the day.

16th. Last night we had the full illumination of all the streets.—The assembly was held at the prætor's, where there was an elegant entertainment and a concert.— Pacherotti, the first man of the opera, distinguished himself very much. I think he he is one of the moſt agreeable ſingers I have ever heard; and am perſuaded, that in a few years, he will be very celebrated. Campanucci, the ſecond ſoprano, is, I think, preferable to moſt that I have heard in Italy; and you will the more eaſily believe this, when I inform you, that he is engaged for next winter, to be the firſt ſinger in the great opera at Rome. Is it not ſtrange, that the capital of all Italy; and, for the fine arts, (as it formerly was for arms) the capital of the world, ſhould condeſcend to chuſe its firſt opera-performer from amongſt the ſubalterns of a remote Sicilian ſtage?

You will believe, that with two ſuch ſopranos as theſe, and Gabrieli for the firſt woman, the opera here will not be a deſpicable one. It is to begin in a few days, notwithſtanding the extreme heat of the ſeaſon; ſo fond are the people here of theſe entertainments.

Their

SICILY AND MALTA.

Their opera dancers are thofe you had laſt year at London: they are juſt arrived, and the people are by no means pleaſed with them. We faw them this morning at the rehearſal; and, to their great furpriſe, addreſſed them in Engliſh. You cannot imagine how happy they were to fee us. Poor fouls! I was delighted to hear with what warmth of gratitude and affection they fpoke of England. There is a mother and two daughters; the youngeſt pretty, but the eldeſt, the firſt dancer, appears a fenſible, modeſt, well-behaved girl;—more fo than is common with thefe fort of people. Speaking of England, fhe faid, with a degree of warmth, that her good treatment in general could hardly infpire, that in her life fhe never left any country with fo fore a heart; and had fhe only enjoyed her health, all the world fhould never have torn her away from it.—She feemed affected when fhe faid this.—I acknowledged

the

the honour she did the English nation; but alleged that these sentiments, and the manner in which they were uttered, could scarcely proceed from a *general love* of the country.—She answered me with a smile, but at the same time I could observe the tear in her eye.—At that instant we were interrupted; however, I shall endeavour, if possible, to learn her story; for I am persuaded there is one: perhaps you may know it, as I dare say it is no secret in London.

But I have got quite away from my subject, and had forgot that I sat down to give you an account of the feast.—Indeed, I will own, it is a kind of subject I by no means like to write upon;—I almost repent that I had undertaken it, and am heartily glad it is now over.—It does very well to see shows; but their description is of all things on earth the most insipid: for words and writing convey

ideas

ideas only by a flow and regular kind of progress; and while we gain one, we generally lose another, so that the fancy seldom embraces the whole;—but when a thousand objects strike you at once, the imagination is filled and satisfied.

The great procession that closes the festival began at ten o'clock—It only differed from other processions in this, that besides all the priests, friars, and religious orders of the city, there were placed at equal distances from each other ten lofty machines made of wood and pasteboard, ornamented in an elegant manner, representing temples, tabernacles, and a variety of beautiful pieces of architecture.—These are furnished by the different convents and religious fraternities, who vie with each other in the richness and elegance of the work. Some of them are not less than sixty feet high.——They are filled with figures

figures of faints and of angels, made of wax, fo natural and fo admirably well painted, that many of them feemed really to be alive. All thefe figures are prepared by the nuns, and by them dreffed out in rich robes of gold and filver tiffue.

We were a good deal amufed this morning to fee them returning home in coaches to their refpective nunneries.—At firft we took them for ladies in their gala drefs, going out to vifit the churches, which we were told was the cuftom, and began to pull off our hats as they went paft.— Indeed, we were led into this blunder by fome of our friends, who carried us out on purpofe; and as they faw the coaches approach, told us, This is the Princefs of fuch a thing:—there is the Dutchefs of fuch another thing;—and, in fhort, we had made half a dozen of our beft bows, (to the no fmall entertainment of thefe wags) before

before we difcovered the trick.—They now infift upon it, that we are good Catholics, for all this morning we had been bowing to faints and angels.

A great filver box, containing the bones of St. Rofolia, clofed the proceffion. It was carried by thirty-fix of the moft refpectable burgeffes of the city, who look upon this as the greateft honour. The archbifhop walked behind it, giving his benediction to the people as he paffed.

No fooner had the proceffion finifhed the tour of the great fquare, before the prætor's palace, than the fountain in the centre, one of the largeft and fineft in Europe, was converted into a fountain of fire; throwing it up on all fides, and making a beautiful appearance. It only lafted for a few minutes, and was extinguifhed by a vaft explofion, which concluded the whole. As this was altogether unex-

unexpected, it produced a fine effect, and surprised the spectators more than any of the great fireworks had done.

There was a mutual and friendly congratulation ran through the whole assembly, which soon after parted; and this morning every thing has once more reassumed its natural form and order;— and I assure you, we were not more happy at the opening of the festival, than we are now at its conclusion. Every body was fatigued and exhausted by the perpetual feasting, watching, and dissipation of these five days. However, upon the whole, we have been much delighted with it, and may with truth pronounce, that the entertainments of the feast of St. Rosolia are much beyond those of the holy week at Rome; of the Ascension, at Venice; or, indeed, any other festival we have ever been witness of.

I believe

I believe I did not tell you, that about ten or twelve days ago, as the time we had appointed for our return to Naples was elapfed, we had hired a fmall veffel, and provided every thing for our departure: we had even taken leave of the viceroy, and received our paffports. Our baggage and fea-ftore was already on board, when we were fet upon by our friends, and folicited with fo much earneftnefs and cordiality, to give them another fortnight, that we found it impoffible to refufe it; and in confequence difcharged our veffel, and fent for our trunks.—I fhould not have mentioned this, were it not to fhew you how much more attention is paid to ftrangers here than in moft places on the continent.

We reckon ourfelves much indebted to them for having obliged us to prolong our ftay; as, independent of the amufements of the feftival, we have met with fo much

hofpi-

hospitality and urbanity, that it is now with the most sincere regret we find ourselves obliged to leave them. Indeed, had we brought our clothes and books from Naples, it is hard to say how long we might have stayed.

We have sent to engage a vessel, but probably shall not sail for five or six days. Adieu.

LETTER XXXI.

Palermo, July 19th.

WE have now had time to inquire a little into fome of the antiquities of this ifland, and have found feveral people, particularly the prince of Torremuzzo, who have made this the great object of their ftudy. However, I find we muft wade through oceans of fiction, before we can arrive at any thing certain or fatiffactory.

Moft of the Sicilian authors agree in deriving their origin from Ham, or as they called him, Cham, the fon of Noah, who, they pretend, is the fame with Saturn. They tell you that he built a great city, which from him was named Camefena. There have been violent difputes about the
Vol. II.   R   fituation

situation of this city:—Berofo fuppofes it to have flood, where Camarina was afterwards founded, and that this was only a corruption of its primitive name. But Guarneri, Carrera, and others, combat this opinion, and affirm, that Camefena flood near the foot of Ætna, between Aci and Cattania, almoft oppofite to thefe three rocks that ftill bear the name of the Cyclops.—Indeed Carrera mentions an infcription that he had feen in a ruin near Aci, fuppofed to have been the fepulchre of Acis, which he thinks puts this matter out of doubt. Thefe are his words: " Hæc eft infcriptio vetuftæ cujufdam tabellæ repertæ in pyramide fepulchri Acis, ex fragmentis vetuftiffimæ Chamefenæ, urbis hodie Acis, conditæ a Cham, gigantum principe, etiam nuncupato Saturno Chamefeno, in promontorio Xiphonio, ubi adhuc hodie vifuntur folo æquata antiqua veftigia, et ruinæ dictæ urbis et arcis in infula prope Scopulos,

Cyclopum,

Cyclopum, et retinet adhuc fincopatum nomen La Gazzena."

This fame Cham they tell you was a very great fcoundrel, and that *efenus*, which fignified infamous, was added to his name, only to denote his character. Fazzello fays, he married his own fifter, who was called Rhea; that Ceres was the fruit of this marriage; that fhe did not inherit the vices of her father, but reigned over Sicily with great wifdom and moderation. That fhe taught her fubjects the method of making bread and wine, the materials for which their ifland produced fpontaneoufly in great abundance. That her daughter Proferpine was of equal beauty and virtue with herfelf. That Orius king of Epirus had demanded her in marriage, and on a refufal, carried her off by force; which gave occafion to the wild imagination of Greece to invent the fable of the rape of Proferpine by Pluto king of Hell, this

Orius being of a morose and gloomy disposition.

Ceres has ever been the favourite deity of the Sicilians. She chose her seat of empire in the centre of the island, on the top of a high hill called Enna, where she founded the city of that name. It is still a considerable place, and is now called Castragiovanni; but little or nothing remain of the ruins of Enna.

Cicero gives a particular account of this place. He says from its situation in the centre of the island, it was called *Umbilicus Siciliæ*, and describes it as one of the most beautiful and fertile spots in the world. The temple of Ceres at Enna was renowned all over the heathen world, and pilgrimages were made to it, as they are at present to Loretto. Fazzello says, it was held in such veneration, that when the city was surprised and pillaged by the slaves and barbarians,

barians, they did not prefume to touch this facred temple, although it contained more riches than all the city befides.

There have been violent difputes amongft the Sicilian authors, whether Proferpine was carried off near the city of Enna, or that of Ætna, which ftood at the foot of that mountain, but it is of mighty little confequence, and more refpect, I think, is to be paid to the fentiments of Cicero, who gives it in favour of Enna, than the whole of them. Diodorus too is of the fame opinion, and his defcription of this place is almoft in the very words as that of Cicero. They both paint it as a perfect paradife; abounding in beautiful groves, clear fprings and rivulets, and like Ætna, covered with a variety of flowers at all feafons of the year. To thefe authorities, if you pleafe you may add that of Milton, who compares it to paradife itfelf:

———Nor

———— Nor that fair field
Of Enna, where Proserpine gathering flowers,
Herself a fairer flower, by gloomy Dis
Was gathered.

If you want to have a fuller account of this place you will find it in Cicero's pleadings against Verres, and in the fifth book of Diodorus—I have conversed with several gentlemen who have been there; they assure me that it still answers in a great measure to the description of these authors. —Medals, I am told, are still found, with an elegant figure of Ceres, and an ear of wheat for the reverse; but I have not been able to procure any of them.

There was another temple in Sicily not less celebrated than this one of Ceres.—It was dedicated to Venus Erecina, and, like the other too, was built on the summit of a high mountain. The ancient name of this mountain was Eryx, or as the Sicilians

cilians call it Erice, but it is now called St. Juliano. Both mountain and temple are often mentioned by the Greek and Latin hiſtorians, and happily the Sicilian ones have no diſpute about its ſituation or origin, which they make to be almoſt as ancient as that of Ceres.—Diodorus ſays, that Dedalus, after his flight from Crete, was hoſpitably received here, and by his wonderful ſkill in architecture added greatly to the beauty of this temple. He enriched it with many fine pieces of ſculpture, but particularly with the figure of a ram of ſuch exquiſite workmanſhip that it appeared to be alive. This, I think, is likewiſe mentioned by Cicero.

Æneas too in his voyage from Troy to Italy, landed in this part of the iſland, and according to Diodorus and Thucydides, made rich preſents to this temple; but Virgil is not ſatisfied with this; he muſt raiſe the piety of his hero ſtill higher, and, in opposition to all the historians, makes Æneas the founder of the temple*. Its fame and glory continued to increase for many ages; and it was still held in greater veneration by the Romans, than it had been by the Greeks. Fazzello says, and quotes the authority of Strabo, that seventeen cities of Sicily were laid under tribute, to raise a sufficient revenue to support the dignity, and enormous expences of this temple. Two hundred soldiers were appointed for its guard, and the number of its priests, priestesses, and ministers male and female, were incredible.

At certain seasons of the year, great numbers of pigeons, which were supposed to be the attendants of Venus, used to pass betwixt Africa and Italy; and resting for

---

* Tum vicina astris Erycino in vertice sede,
Fundatur Veneri Idaliæ, tumuloque sacerdos
Et lucus late sacer additur Anchisæo.

†

some days on mount Eryx, and round this temple, it was then imagined by the people that the goddess herself was there in person; and on these occasions, he says, they worshipped her with all their might. —Festivals were instituted in honour of the deity, and the most modest woman was only looked upon as a prude, that refused to comply with the rites. However, there were not many complaints of this kind; and it has been alleged, that the ladies of Eryx were sometimes seen looking out for the pigeons long before they arrived; and that they used to scatter peas about the temple to make them stay as long as possible.

Venus was succeeded in her possessions of Eryx by St. Juliano, who now gives his name both to the city and mountain; and indeed he has a very good title, for when the place was closely besieged, the Sicilians tell you, he appeared on the walls armed
cap-

cap-a-pie, and frightened the enemy to fuch a degree, that they inftantly took to their heels, and left him ever fince in quiet poffeffion of it.—It would have been long before Venus and her pigeons could have done as much for them.

Many medals are found in the neighbourhood, but there is not the leaft veftige of this celebrated temple.—Some marbles with infcriptions and engravings that have been found deep below ground are almoft the only remaining monuments of its exiftence. Suetonius fays, that it had even fallen to ruins before the time of Tiberius; but as Venus was the favourite divinity of that emperor, he had ordered it to be magnificently repaired: however, it is fomewhat difficult to reconcile this with Strabo's account; who tells us, that even before his time it had been totally abandoned; and indeed this feems moft probable, as every veftige of it has now difappeared,

peared, which is not commonly the cafe with the great works of the age of Tiberius.

Æneas landed at the port of Drepanum, at the foot of this mountain. Here he loft his father Anchifes; in honour of whom, on his return from Carthage about a year after, he celebrated the games that make fo great a figure in the Æneid, which Virgil introduces with a good deal of addrefs as a compliment to the piety of Auguftus, who had inftituted games of the fame kind in honour of Julius Cæfar, his father by adoption.

It is fingular, that Virgil's account of this part of Sicily fhould be fo very different from that of Homer, when there was fo fhort a fpace, only a few months, between the times that their two heroes vifited it.—Indeed, Virgil feems to have followed

lowed the historians, in his conduct of this part of his poem, more than the sentiments of Homer; who makes this very country where Æneas was so hospitably received, the habitation of Polyphemus and the Cyclops, where Ulysses lost so many of his companions, and himself made so very narrow an escape. The island of Licosia where he moored his fleet, lay very near the port of Drepanum, and Homer describes the adventure of Polyphemus to have happened on the shore of Sicily, opposite to that island. Virgil has taken the liberty to change the scene of action, as he was better acquainted both with the geography and history of the country than Homer; and perhaps with a good deal of propriety places it at the foot of mount Ætna. I am afraid there is not so much propriety in his changing the action itself, and contradicting the account that Homer gives of it. For Ulysses says that Polyphemus devoured four

of

of his companions; but that he, by his addrefs, faved all the reft, and was himfelf the laft that efcaped out of the cave. Now Virgil makes Ulyffes to have told a lie, for he affirms that he left Achemenides behind him; and Achemenides too gives a different account of this affair from Ulyffes: he affures Æneas, that Polyphemus devoured only two of his companions; after which they put out his eye, *(acuto telo)* with a fharp weapon; which rather gives the idea of a fpear or javelin, than that of a great beam of wood made red hot in the fire, as Homer defcribes it. But there are many fuch paffages.—Don't you think they feem either to indicate a negligence in Virgil; or a want of deference for his mafter? neither of which, I believe, he has ever been accufed of.

The Sicilian authors are by no means pleafed with Virgil for making Æneas the founder

founder of this temple of Venus Erecina. They will only allow that the colony which he was obliged to leave there, after the burning of his ships, did, in honour of his mother Venus, build the city of Eryx around her temple: but they all insist upon it, that the temple was built by Eryx, or as they call him Erice, another son of Venus, but much older than Æneas; the same that was found to be so equal a match for Hercules, but was at last killed by him, at a boxing match near the foot of this mountain. The spot where this is supposed to have happened, still retains the name of *(il campo di Hercole)* the field of Hercules. Through the whole fifth book of the Æneid, this Eryx is styled the brother of Æneas; and, in his account of the games, Virgil introduces those very gauntlets with which he fought with Hercules, *(in hoc ipso littore)* in this very field. The sight of which, from their enormous fize, aftonifhes the whole hoft, and frightens the champion Dares fo much that he refufes to fight.

Adieu. The opera begins in two days; after which, I think, we fhall foon take leave of Sicily.

Ever yours.

LETTER XXXII.

Palermo, July 21st.

YESTERDAY we walked up to the Monte Pelegrino to pay our respects to St. Rosolia, and thank her for the variety of entertainment she has afforded us. It is one of the most fatiguing expeditions I ever made in my life. The mountain is extremely high, and so uncommonly steep, that the road up to it is very properly termed *la Scala*, or the Stair: before the discovery of St. Rosolia, it was looked upon as almost inaccessible, but they have now at a vast expence cut out a road, over precipices that were almost perpendicular. We found the saint lying in her grotto, in the very same attitude in which she is said to have been discovered; her head reclining gently upon her hand, and a crucifix before her. This is a statue of the finest white marble,

marble, and of moſt exquiſite workmanſhip. It is placed in the inner part of the
cavern, on the very ſame ſpot where St.
Roſolia expired. It is the figure of a lovely
young girl of about fifteen, in an act of
devotion. The artiſt has found means to
throw ſomething that is extremely touch-
ing, into the countenance and air of this
beautiful ſtatue. I never in my life ſaw one
that affected me ſo much, and am not ſurpriſed that it ſhould have captivated the
hearts of the people. It is covered with a
robe of beaten gold, and is adorned with
ſome valuable jewels. The cave is of a
conſiderable extent, and extremely damp,
ſo that the poor little ſaint muſt have had
very cold uncomfortable quarters. They
have built a church around it; and appointed prieſts to watch over theſe precious
relics, and receive the offerings of pilgrims
that viſit them.

An inſcription graved by the hand of
St. Roſolia herſelf, was found in a cave in

mount Quesquina, at a considerable distance from this mountain. It is said that she was disturbed in her retreat there, and had wandered from thence to mount Pelegrino, as a more retired and inaccessible place. I shall copy it exactly, as it is preserved in the poor little saint's own Latin.

EGO ROSOLIA
SINIBALDI QUISQUI-
NE ET ROSARUM
DOMINI FILIA AMORE
DEI MEI JESU
CHRISTI
IN HOC
ANTRO HABITA-
RI DECREVI.

After St. Rosolia was scared from the cave where this inscription was found, she was never more heard of, till her bones were found about five hundred years after, in this spot.

The prospect from the top of mount Pelegrino is beautiful and extensive. Most of the Lipari islands are discovered in a very clear day, and likewise a large portion of mount

mount Ætna, although at the diftance of almoft the whole length of Sicily. The Bagaria too, and the Colle, covered over with a number of fine country-houfes and gardens, make a beautiful appearance. The city of Palermo ftands within lefs than two miles of the foot of the mountain, and is feen to great advantage. Many people went to this mountain during the time of the great illumination, from whence they pretend it has a fine effect: but this unfortunately we neglected.

Near the middle of the mountain, and not far from its fummit, there ftill appears fome remains of a celebrated caftle, the origin of which the Sicilian authors carry back to the moft remote antiquity. Maffa fays, it is fuppofed to have been built in the reign of Saturn immediately after the flood; for in the time of the earlieft Carthaginian wars, it was already much refpected on account of its venerable antiquity.

quity.—It was then a place of strength, and is often mentioned by the Greek historians. Diodorus says, in his twenty-third book, that Hamilcar kept possession of it for three years, against all the power of the Romans, who with an army of forty thousand men attempted in vain to dislodge him.

The situation of Palermo is seen, I think, to more advantage from the monte Pelegrino than from any where else. This beautiful city stands near the extremity of a kind of natural amphitheatre, formed by high and rocky mountains; but the country that lies betwixt the city and these mountains, is one of the richest and most beautiful spots in the world. The whole appears a magnificent garden, filled with fruit-trees of every species, and watered by clear fountains and rivulets, that form a variety of windings through this delightful plain.— From the singularity of this situation, as well as from the richness of the soil, Palermo

lermo has had many flattering epithets beſtowed upon it; particularly by the poets, who have denominated it *Conca d'oro*, The Golden Shell, which is at once expreſſive both of its ſituation and richneſs. It has likewiſe been ſtyled *Aurea Valle*, *Hortus Siciliæ*, &c. and to include all theſe together, the laſting term of *Felix* has been added to its name, by which you will find it diſtinguiſhed even in the maps.

Many of the etymologiſts allege, that it is from the richneſs of this valley that it had its original name of *Panormus*, which, in the old Greek language, they pretend, ſignified All a garden: but others ſay there is no occaſion for ſtraining ſignifications, and aſſert, with more appearance of plauſibility, that it was called *Pan-ormus*, from the ſize and conveniency of its harbours; one of which is recorded anciently to have extended into the very centre of the city. And this is the account Diodorus gives of it; it was called

called Panormus, fays he, becaufe its harbour even penetrated to the very innermoft parts of the city. Panormus in the Greek language fignifying All a port. And Procopius, in his hiftory of the wars of the Goths, affures us, that in the time of Belifarius, the port was deep enough for that general to run his fhips up to the very walls of the city, and give the affault from them. It is not now fo well entitled to this name as it was formerly. Thefe harbours have been almoft entirely deftroyed and filled up; moft probably I think by the violent torrents from the mountains that furround it; which are recorded fometimes to have laid wafte great part of the city. Fazzello fpeaks of an inundation of which he was an eye-witnefs, that came down from the mountains with fuch fury, that they thought the city would have been entirely fwept away. He fays, it burft down the wall near to the royal palace, and bore away every thing that oppofed its paffage; churches,

churches, convents, houses, to the number of two thousand, and drowned upwards of three thousand people.—Now the fragments and ruins carried to the sea by such a torrent alone, would be sufficient to fill up a little harbour, so that we are not to be surprised, that these capacious ports, for which it had been so much celebrated, no longer exist.

Next to Chameseno, Palermo is generally supposed to be the most ancient city in the island. Indeed, there still remain some monuments that carry back its origin to the times of the most remote antiquity. A bishop of Lucera has wrote on this subject. He is clearly of opinion, that Palermo was founded in the days of the first patriarchs. You will laugh at this;—so did I;—but the bishop does not go to work upon conjecture only: he supports his opinion with such proofs, as I own to you, staggered me a good deal. A Chaldean

dean infcription was difcovered about fix hundred years ago, on a block of white marble; it was in the reign of William II. who ordered it to be tranflated into Latin and Italian. The bifhop fays, there are many fragments in Palermo with broken infcriptions in this language; and feems to think it beyond a doubt, that the city was founded by the Chaldeans, in the very early ages of the world. This is the literal tranflation:——" During the time that Ifaac,
" the fon of Abraham, reigned in the valley
" of Damafcus, and Efau, the fon of Ifaac,
" in Idumea, a great multitude of Hebrews,
" accompanied by many of the people of
" Damafcus, and many Phœnicians, coming
" into this triangular ifland, took up their
" habitation in this moft beautiful place,
" to which they gave the name of Panor-
" mus."

The bifhop tranflates another Chaldean infcription, which is indeed a great curiofity.

fity. It is ftill preferved, though not with that care that fo valuable a monument of antiquity deferves. It is placed over one of the old gates of the city, and when that gate falls to ruin, it will probably be for ever loft. The tranflation is in Latin, but I fhall give it you in Englifh:——" There
" is no other God but one God. There is
" no other power but this fame God. There
" is no other conqueror but this God whom
" we adore. The commander of this tower
" is Saphu, the fon of Eliphar, fon of Efau,
" brother of Jacob, fon of Ifaac, fon of
" Abraham. The name of the tower is
" Baych, and the name of the neighbour-
" ing tower is Pharat."

Thefe two infcriptions feem to reflect a mutual light upon each other. Fazzello has preferved them both, and remarks upon this laft, that it appears evidently from it, that the tower of Baych was built antecedent to the time of Saphu, (or, as we tranflate it, Zephu) who is only mentioned as commander of the tower, but not as its founder.

Part of the ruins of this tower ſtill remain, and many more Chaldean inſcriptions have been found amongſt them, but ſo broken and mangled, that little could be made of them. Fazzello is in great indignation at ſome maſons he found demoliſhing theſe precious relics, and complains bitterly of it to the ſenate, whom he with juſtice upbraids for their negligence and indifference.

Converſing on this ſubject t'other night with a gentleman who is well verſed in the antiquities of this place, I took the liberty of objecting to the Greek etymology, Pan-ormus, it appearing extremely abſurd to give a Greek name to the city long before the exiſtence of the Greek nation: I added, that I was a good deal ſurpriſed

surprised Fazzello had not attempted to account for this seeming absurdity. He allowed the apparent validity of the objection, and blamed Fazzello for his negligence; but assured me, that Pan-ormus, or something very nearly of the same sound, signified in the Chaldean language, and likewise in the Hebrew, a paradise, or delicious garden; and that the Greeks probably finding it so applicable, never thought of changing its name. This I was in no capacity to contradict.—He added too, that Panormus was likewise an Arabic word, and signified *This water*; which probably was the reason that the Saracens did not change its name, as they have done that of almost every thing else; as this is as applicable and as expressive of the situation of Palermo, as any of the other etymologies; it being surrounded on all sides with beautiful fountains of the purest water, the natural consequence of the vicinity of the mountains.

Pray

Pray shew this letter to our friend Mr. Crofts, and defire his fentiments on thefe etymologies and antiquities. Tell him I have not forgot his commiffion, and fhall procure him all the oldeft and moft unintelligible books in Palermo; but I muft beg, for the repofe and tranquillity of mankind, that he will not republifh them. On thefe conditions, I fend him a moft valuable fragment: it is part of a Chaldean infcription that has been exactly copied from a block of white marble found in the ruins of the tower Baych.—I own I fhould like much to fee it tranflated : the people here have as yet made nothing of it : and we were in no capacity to affift them.

SICILY AND MALTA. 269

On confulting the Bible, I find, that in our tranflation this fon of Efau is called Eliphaz, and Eliphaz's fon, who was captain of this tower, Zepho. The variation of the names you fee is but trifling. It is not improbable that the other tower, Pharat, by a fmall variation of the fame kind, has

has been named from their coufin, Pharez, the fon of Judah, who got the ftart of his brother Zarah. You will find the ftory at the end of the thirty-eighth chapter of Genefis. The thirty-feventh chapter will give you fome account of Eliphar and Saphu: but I can find no etymology for the name of the tower Baych. I dare fay Mr. Crofts can tell you what it means.— Pharez fignifies a breach; a very inaufpicious name one would think for a tower. Adieu. The weather has become exceeding hot. The thermometer is at 80.

Ever yours.

LETTER XXXIII.

Palermo, July 24th.

IN the course of our acquaintance with some gentlemen of sense and observation in this place, we have learned many things concerning the island, that perhaps may be worthy of your attention; and as this day is so hot that I cannot go out, I shall endeavour to recollect some of them, both for your amusement and my own. The thermometer is up at $81\frac{1}{2}$.—So you may judge of the situation of our northern constitutions.

There is one thing, however, that I have always observed in these southern climates; that although the degree of heat is much greater than with us, yet it is not commonly attended with that weight and

and oppreffion of fpirits that generally accompany our fultry days in fummer.—I am fure, that in fuch a day as this, in England, we fhould be panting for breath; and no mortal would think either of reading or writing.—That is not the cafe here; I never was in better fpirits in my life: Indeed I believe the quantities of ice we eat may contribute a good deal towards it; for I find, that in a very violent heat, there is no fuch cordial to the fpirits as ice, or a draught of ice-water: it is not only from the cold it communicates, but, like the cold bath, from the fuddennefs of that communication, it braces the ftomach, and gives a new tone to the fibres.—It is ftrange that this piece of luxury (in my opinion the greateft of all, and perhaps the only healthy one) fhould ftill be fo much neglected with us.

I knew an Englifh lady at Nice, who in a fhort time was cured of a threatening confumption, only by a free indulgence in the ufe of ices; and I am perfuaded, that in fkilful hands, few remedies would be more effectual in many of our ftomach and inflammatory complaints, as hardly any thing has a ftronger or more immediate effect upon the whole frame; and furely our adminiftering of warm drinks and potions in thefe complaints tend often to nourifh the difeafe.—It is the common practice here, in inflammatory fevers, to give quantities of ice-water to drink; nay, fo far have they carried it, that Dr. Sanghes, a celebrated Sicilian phyfician, covered over the breaft and belly of his patients with fnow or ice; and they affure us, in many cafes, with great fuccefs.— But, indeed, I ought in juftice to add, that this phyfician's practice has not been generally adopted.

Perhaps it is from the prefent benefit I find from ice, that I have faid fo much in favour

favour of it; for I am fully perſuaded, that if I had not a quantity of it ſtanding here below the table, I ſhould very ſoon be obliged to give up writing, and go to bed; but whenever I begin to flag, another glaſs is ſure to ſet me to rights again.

I was going to give you ſome account of the fiſheries of this iſland.

The catching of the tunny-fiſh conſtitutes one of the principal Sicilian amuſements during the ſummer months; and the curing and ſending them to foreign markets makes one of the greateſt branches of their commerce.—We were invited yeſterday by the Prince Sperlinga to a party of tunny-fiſhing; but the violence of the heat prevented it.

Theſe fiſh do not make their appearance in the Sicilian ſeas till towards the latter end of May; at which time, the *Tonnaros*, as they call them, are prepared for their reception. This is a kind of aquatic caftle, formed, at a great expence, of ftrong nets, faftened to the bottom of the fea by anchors and heavy leaden weights.

Thefe tonnaros are erected in the paffages amongft the rocks and iflands that are moft frequented by the tunny-fifh. They take care to fhut up with nets the entry into thefe paffages, all but one little opening, which is called the outward gate of the tonnaro. This leads into the firft apartment, or, as they call it, the hall. As foon as the fifh have got into the hall, the fifhermen, who ftand fentry in their boats during the feafon, fhut the outer door, which is no more than letting down a fmall piece of net, which effectually prevents the tunny from returning by the way they came. They then open the inner door of the hall, which leads to the fecond apartment, which they call the antichamber,

chamber, and, by making a noife on the furface of the water, they foon drive the tunny-fifh into it. As foon as the whole have got into the antichamber, the inner door of the hall is again fhut, and the outer door is opened for the reception of more company.

Some tonnaros have a great number of apartments, with different names to them all; the faloon, the parlour, the dining-room, &c.; but the laft apartment is always ftyled *la Camera della Morte*, The chamber of Death: this is compofed of ftronger nets and heavier anchors than the others.

As foon as they have collected a fufficient number of tunny-fifh, they are driven from all the other apartments into the chamber of death; when the flaughter begins. The fifhermen, and often the gentlemen too, armed with a kind of fpear or harpoon, attack the poor defenceless animals on all sides; which now giving themselves up to despair, dash about with great force and agility, throwing the water over all the boats; and tearing the nets to pieces, they often knock out their brains against the rocks or anchors, and sometimes even against the boats of their enemies.

You see there is nothing very generous or manly in this sport.—The taking of the *Pesce Spada*, or sword-fish, is a much more noble diversion: no art is made use of to ensnare him; but with a small harpoon, fixed to a long line, they attack him in the open seas, and will often strike him at a very considerable distance. It is exactly the whale-fishing in miniature. The Sicilian fishermen (who are abundantly superstitious) have a Greek sentence which they make use of as a charm to bring him near their boats. This is the only bait they

they use, and they pretend that it is of wonderful efficacy, and absolutely obliges him to follow them; but if unfortunately he should overhear them speak a word of Italian, he plunges under water immediately, and will appear no more.

As these fish are commonly of a great size and strength, they will sometimes run for hours after they are struck, and afford excellent sport.—I have seen them with a sword four or five feet long, which gives them a formidable appearance in the water, particularly after they are wounded. The flesh of these animals is excellent; it is more like beef than fish, and the common way of dressing it is in steaks.

The fishing of the *pesce Spada* is most considerable in the sea of Messina, where they have likewise great quantities of eels, particularly the *Morena*, so much esteemed amongst the Romans, which I think is indeed the finest fish I ever eat.

But it is not only their large fish that they strike with harpoons; they have the same method of taking mullet, dories, a kind of mackarel, and many other species; but this is always performed in the night. As soon as it is dark, two men get into a small boat; one of them holds a lighted torch over the surface of the water, the other stands with his harpoon ready poized in his hand. The light of the torch soon brings the fish to the surface, when the harpooner immediately strikes them. I have seen great quantities killed in this manner, both here and at Naples. A large fleet of boats employed in this kind of fishing make a beautiful appearance on the water, in a fine summer night.

The coral fishery is chiefly practised at Trapani: they have invented a machine there,

there, which anfwers the purpofe much beyond their expectations. This is only a great crofs of wood, to the centre of which is fixed a heavy hard ftone, capable of carrying the crofs to the bottom. Pieces of fmall net are tied to each limb of the crofs, which is poized horizontally by a rope, and let down into the water. As foon as they feel it touch the bottom, the rope is made faft to the boat. They then row about all over the coral beds: The confequence of which is, the great ftone breaks off the coral from the rocks, and it is immediately entangled in the nets.— Since this invention the coral fifhery has turned out to confiderable account.

The people of Trepani are efteemed the moft ingenious of the ifland; they are the authors of many ufeful and ornamental inventions. An artift there, has lately difcovered a method of making Cameios, which are a perfect imitation of the ancient ones

ones engraved on the onyx. They are done on a kind of hard shell from pastes of the best antiques, and so admirably executed, that it is often difficult to distinguish the ancient from the modern. These set in gold, are generally worn as bracelets, and are at present in high estimation amongst the ladies of quality here. Mrs. Hamilton * procured a pair of them last year, and carried them to Naples, where they have been much admired. Commissions were immediately sent over, and the man has now more business than he can manage; however, we have been fortunate enough to procure a few pairs of them for our friends. I have seen cameios that have cost two hundred guineas, that could scarce be distinguished from one of these.

The difficulties under which the poor Sicilians labour, from the extreme oppres-

---

* Now lady Hamilton.

sion of their government, obliges them sometimes to invent branches of commerce that nature seems to have denied them, as they are not allowed to enjoy those she has bestowed.—The sugar-cane was very much cultivated in this island, but the duties imposed were so enormous, that it has been almost abandoned.—But their crops of wheat alone, were they under a free government, would soon be sufficient to render this little nation one of the richest and most flourishing in the world; for even in the wretched state of cultivation it is in at present, one good crop, I am told, is sufficient to maintain the island for seven years. You will be a good deal surprised, after this, to hear that the exportation of this commodity has been prohibited for these several years past; at least to all such as are not able to pay most exorbitantly for that privilege. The consequence is, that corn has become a drug. The common price of the salma, which is

two

two loads, was about thirty-one shillings; at present it is reduced to five shillings and six-pence, and there is a probability that it will still fall lower.

This crop, which has been very abundant, I am told, in many places they have hardly been at the pains to gather in, as there is little probability of this cruel prohibition being removed. The farmers are already ruined, and the ruin of their masters must inevitably follow. This is the method the ministry of Naples, or rather that of Spain, has taken to humble the pride of the Sicilian barons, whose power they pretend is still very extensive, and their jurisdiction absolute; most of them possessing a right of life and death in their own domain. However, there is a probability that they will soon be obliged to relinquish their privileges. The complaint is universal, and if the ministry persevere in these rigorous measures, there must

must either be a revolt, or they must soon be reduced to a state of poverty as well as of servitude. I believe indeed most of them would readily embrace any plausible scheme, to shake off their yoke; as in general they appear to be people of great sensibility, with high notions of honour and liberty.

Talking of the natural riches of their island,—Yes, say they, if these were displayed, you would have reason indeed to speak of them. Take a look of these mountains,—they contain rich veins of every metal, and many of the Roman mines still remain;—but to what end should we explore them?—It is not we that should reap the profit.—Nay, a discovery of any thing very rich might possibly prove the ruin of its possessor.—No, —in our present situation the hidden treasures of the island must ever remain a profound secret.—Were we happy enough to enjoy the blessings of your constitution,

you

you might call us rich indeed. Many hidden doors of opulence would then be opened, which now are not even thought of, and we ſhould ſoon re-aſſume our ancient name and conſequence; but at preſent we are nothing.

This is the language that ſome of the firſt people amongſt them hold with us. However, they ſtill boaſt that they retain more of the feudal government than any nation in Europe. The ſhadow indeed remains, but the ſubſtance is gone long ago. It has long been the objeƈt of the Bourbon miniſtry to reduce the power of the barons in every kingdom. Richlieu began the ſyſtem in France, and it has ever ſince been proſecuted by his ſucceſſors; its influence has now ſpread over the whole of their poſſeſſions in Europe; of which, as this is the moſt remote, it has likewiſe been the longeſt in reaching it.

The

The foundation of the feudal fyftem was firſt laid here by the count Rugiero, about the middle of the eleventh century, immediately after he had driven the Saracens out of the iſland. He divided Sicily into three parts; the firſt, by confent of his army, was given to the church; the fecond he beſtowed upon his officers, and the third he referved for himfelf.

Of thefe three branches, or as they call them *Braccios* (arms), he compofed his parliament, the form of which remains the fame to this day. The *Braccio Militare* is compofed of all the barons of the kingdom, to the number of two hundred and fifty-one, who are ſtill obliged to military fervice: their chief is the prince Butero, who is hereditary prefident of the parliament: for in conformity to the genius of the feudal government fome of the great offices are ſtill hereditary. The three archbifhops, all the bifhops, abbes, priors,

priors, and dignified clergy, amounting to near seventy, form the *Braccio Ecelefiaftico*: The archbifhop of Palermo is their chief. The *Braccio Demaniale* is formed by election, like our houfe of commons: there are forty-three royal cities, ftyled *Demaniale*, that have a right to elect members. Every houfeholder had a vote in this election. Their chief is the member for Palermo; who is likewife prætor (or mayor of the city). He is an officer of the higheft rank, and his power is very extenfive; inferior only to that of the viceroy; in whofe abfence, the greateft part of the authority devolves upon him. He has a company of grenadiers for his body-guard and receives the title of excellency.

The prætor, together with fix fenators, who are ftyled patricians, have the management of the civil government of the city He is appointed every year, by the king, or by the viceroy, which is the fame thing

thing; for I don't find that the people any longer exercife even the form of giving their votes: fo that the very fhadow of liberty has now difappeared as well as the fubftance.—You may judge of the fituation of liberty in a kingdom, where all courts civil and criminal are appointed by regal authority, and where all offices are conferred only by the will of the fovereign, and depend entirely upon his caprice.

I own I feel moft fincerely for the Sicilians, who, I think, are poffeffed of many admirable qualities. But the fpirit of every nation muft infallibly fink, under an oppreffive and tyrannical government.—Their fpirit however has in a great meafure kept them free from one branch of tyranny, the moft dreadful of all, that of the inquifition. The kings of Spain wanted to eftablifh it in its full force; but the barons, accuftomed to exercife defpotic government themfelves, could not bear the thoughts of

VOL. II.   U   be-

becoming slaves to a set of ignorant Spanish priests: and, I believe, they took the only way that was left to avoid it. Every inquisitor that pretended to more zeal than they thought became him, was immediately assassinated; particularly if he presumed to interfere with the conduct or sentiments of the nobility. This soon took off the edge of their zeal, and reduced the holy office to a becoming moderation. However, they are extremely circumspect in their conversation about religious matters; and generally advise strangers to be on their guard, as the power of the inquisition, although considerably reduced, is by no means annihilated.

The laws of Sicily are scattered in a great number of volumes; these the king of Sardinia intended to abridge, and collect into one code, but unfortunately he was not long enough in possession of the island, to accomplish this useful work.—
But

But where there is an authority above all laws, laws can be but of little service.

The power of the viceroy is very abfolute; he has not only the command of all the military force in the kingdom, but likewife prefides with unbounded authority in all civil tribunals; and as he is alfo invefted with the legantine power, his fway is equally great in religious matters.

He has the right of nominating to all the great offices in the kingdom; and confirming of all dignities, both civil and ecclefiaftical.

In vifiting the prifons, a ceremony which he performs with great pomp twice a year, he has the power of liberating whatever prifoners he pleafes; of reducing or altering their fentences, their crimes and accufations having firft been read over to him.

Indeed, that there may be some appearance of a regard to law and justice, his counsellor always attends him on these occasions, to mark out the limits of the law.—This is an officer of very high rank, appointed to assist the viceroy in his decisions, where the case may appear intricate or dubious; and always is, or ought to be, one of the ablest lawyers in the island. For the most part, this office has been given to strangers, who are supposed to have no kindred or particular connections here, that in giving their judgment they may be free from all prejudice and partiality. He has free admittance into all courts and tribunals, that he may be the better enabled to give the viceroy an account of their proceedings.

The whole military force of Sicily, amounts at present, from what I can learn, to 9500 men, about 1200 of which are cavalry. Many of their cities and fortresses

treſſes would require a very numerous garriſon to defend them; particularly Meſſina, Syracuſe, and Palermo: but indeed the ſtate of their fortifications, as well as that of their artillery, is ſuch, that (even if they were inclined) they could make but a ſmall defence.

If this iſland were in the hands of a naval power, I think it is evident, that it muſt command the whole Levant trade;— there are ſeveral little ports at each end of it, beſides the great ones of Trapani, Syracuſe, and Meſſina, which lie pretty near the three angles of the triangle. Whatever ſhips had paſſed either of theſe, the others could be apprized of in the ſpace of half an hour, by means of ſignal towers, which the Sicilians have erected all around their iſland to warn them againſt ſudden invaſions from the Barbary ſide. Theſe towers are built on every little promontory, within ſight of each other. Fires are

are always kept ready for lighting, and a perſon is appointed to watch at each of them, ſo that the whole iſland can be alarmed, they aſſure us, in the ſpace of an hour.

By the bye, we have been witneſs here of a practice, that appears to be a very iniquitous one, and in the end, I ſhould think, muſt prove the deſtruction of our Mediterranean trade. Several ſhips have put in at this port with Engliſh colours, but to our ſurpriſe, not one Engliſhman on board. Theſe, I find, they call Bandiere men;—perhaps it is a known practice, although, I own, I was an utter ſtranger to it. They are very numerous in theſe ſeas, and carry on a conſiderable trade through the whole of the Mediterranean, to the great detriment of our own ſhips. Moſt of them belong to Genoa and Sicily, though they paſs under the name of Minorquins. They purchaſe

Medi-

Mediterranean paſsports, I am told, from some of the governors of our garriſons, which entitles them, during the term ſpecified in theſe paſsports, to trade under Engliſh colours. I am aſsured that the number of theſe Bandiere men amounts to ſome hundreds. They have often one or two Engliſh ſailors on board; or at leaſt ſome perſon that ſpeaks the language, to anſwer when they are challenged. Pray can you tell me, if this practice is known in England?

Adieu. The heat has become intolerable, and I am able to write no more;—however, I ſhould not have given it up yet, but my ice is all melted, and I have not the conſcience to ſend out a ſervant for more: I dare ſay, you are very glad of it, and wiſhed it had been melted long ago. If this continues, I believe we ourſelves ſhall be melted. The thermometer is above eighty-

eighty-two, and the heat still seems to increase.—The sea has even become too hot for bathing; and it does not at all refresh us now as it did formerly.

Farewell.

LETTER XXXIV.

Palermo, July 26th.

WE have now got every thing ready for our departure, and if the wind continues favourable, this is probably the laſt letter I ſhall write you from Sicily. However, I had ſtill a great deal more to ſay, both of the Sicilians and their iſland, and ſhall leave them, I aſſure you, with a good deal of regret.

Two chebecks ſailed this morning for Naples. 'We had the offer of a paſſage; but had already engaged a little veſſel for ourſelves.—A young nobleman, the marquis of——, was ſhipped off in one of them, with orders never more to ſet his foot in Palermo. Indeed we are much ſurpriſed that his ſentence is ſo mild, as he

has

has been guilty of a crime which in catholic countries is generally punifhed with the greateft rigour;—no lefs than the debauching a nun.—He met with the young lady at a bathing-place, about thirty miles from this, where fhe had been fent from her convent for the recovery of her health; her mother was along with her, but as the two young people were firft coufins, and had lived together like brother and fifter, the old lady thought there could be no rifk in allowing them their wonted familiarity.

The nun foon recovered her health, grew fat, and returned to her convent. This is about fix or feven months ago; and it is only a few days fince the fatal difcovery was made; but alas, it would conceal no longer. He is banifhed Sicily for life; and his eftate, or the greateft part of it, is confifcated. He may think himfelf happy they have treated him with fo much lenity; Had his jury been compofed of priefts priests and confessors, he must have died, without benefit of clergy; for this is the first mortal sin, for which there is neither atonement nor absolution;—" to lie with a " nun, and yet not be in orders."

The punishment of the poor unfortunate girl is not yet determined; however, I am told, it will be a terrible one: probably confinement in a dungeon for seven or eight years, without any company but a skull and a crucifix; and to live all that time upon bread and water. I saw a nun, at Portallegre in Portugal, that had suffered this very punishment for the same crime.

This story has been kept a profound secret, and if we had not been on a very intimate footing with some people here, we never should have heard of it.

The Sicilians still retain some of the Spanish customs, though nothing of their

gravity

gravity nor taciturnity: the younger sons of the nobility are styled Don by their christened names, and the daughters Donna; like our appellation of lord and lady to the sons and daughters of dukes. The eldest son has commonly the title of count or marquis, but they are not all counts as in France and Germany, where I have seen six counts in one house, and very near twice the number of barons in another.

One of the most common titles here, as well as at Naples, is that of Prince; and although these were only created by Philip II. of Spain, they take rank of all the other nobility, some of whom, particularly the counts, carry their origin as far back as the time of the Normans, and look with great contempt on these upstart Princes. The dukes and marquisses are not so old: the first were created by Charles V, and the second, though an inferior title, by King Alphonso, in the fifteenth century.—

So

So that the dignity of the Sicilian titles may be said to be in the inverse ratio of their antiquities.

The luxury of the people here, like that of the Neapolitans, consists chiefly in their equipages and horses; but by a wise law of the King of Sardinia, which I am surprised should still remain in force, the viceroy alone is allowed to drive in the city with six horses; the prætor, the archbishop, and president of the parliament with four; all the rest of the nobility are restricted to two. But this is only within the gates of Palermo; and when they go to the country, there is none of them that drive with less than four: besides, every family of distinction has at least two or three carriages in daily use; for no man of fashion is so unpolite as to refuse his wife a chariot of her own, of which she has the entire command; (without this the Marino could never subsist) and the upper servants of the first families

families would be juſt as much aſhamed to be ſeen on foot as their maſters.—We took the liberty to ridicule the folly of this practice: they allow of its abſurdity, and wiſh to break through it; but who is to lead the way? We even prevailed with ſome of the young nobility, which I aſſure you was no ſmall condeſcenſion, to walk the ſtreets with us during the illuminations; but even this condeſcenſion ſhewed the folly of the prejudice in a ſtronger light than if they had refuſed us; for they would not be prevailed on to ſtir out, till they had ſent their ſervants about ten yards before them, with large wax flambeaux, although the whole city was in a flame of light. You may believe we did not ſpare them upon this occaſion; but it was all to no purpoſe. However, it is poſſible that we may overlook many cuſtoms of our own, that are not leſs ridiculous; for ridicule for the moſt part is relative, and depends only on time and place.—Perhaps you may remember the
Prince

Prince of Anamaboo;—I should like to hear the account he would give of the English nation in his own country; for some of our cuftoms ftruck him in a ftill more ridiculous light.———Walking out in St. James's Park, in the afternoon, he obferved one of his acquaintance driving in a phaeton with four horfes. The Prince burft into a violent fit of laughing:—When they afked him, what was the matter?—" Vat
" the devil, (faid the Prince in his bad
" Englifh) has that fellow eat fo much
" dinner that now it takes four horfes to
" carry him?——I rode out with him this
" morning, and he was then fo light, that
" van little horfe ran away with him.—He
" muft either be a great fool or a great
" glutton."—Another time they infifted on the Prince going to the play:—He went; but he foon tired of it, and returned to his companions.—" Well, Prince, (faid they)
" what did you fee?"—" Vat did I fee,
" (replied

" (replied he, with the utmoſt contempt) I
" did ſee ſome men playing de fiddle—and
" ſome men playing de fool."

I only infer from this, that it is with ſome degree of caution we ſhould ridicule the cuſtoms of other nations: a Sicilian, perhaps, would laugh with as much juſtice at many of our cuſtoms;—that, for inſtance, of obliging people to drink when they have no inclination to it;—that in the North, of eating Soland geeſe before dinner, to give them an appetite;—that of phyſicians and lawyers wearing enormous wigs, and many others that will naturally occur to you, none of which appear in the leaſt ridiculous to the people that practiſe them; who would no doubt defend them as ſtrenuouſly as the Sicilians do the neceſſity of carrying flambeaux before them during the great illumination.—Indeed, they have juſt now given us an admirable ſpecimen

specimen of some of our ridicules, in one of their opera dances, with which we have been a good deal entertained.

I believe I told you that the dancers are lately come from England: they have brought upon the stage many of the capital London characters: The bucks, the maccaronies, the prigs, the cits, and some others still more respectable: these are well supported, and afford a good deal of laughing. But I am interrupted, otherwise I should have given you a more particular account of them. Adieu. The heat is intolerable; and there is no possibility of walking out.—We complain without reason of our own climate; and King Charles's observation I am persuaded was just; " That there is hardly any climate, where, throughout the year, we can have so much exercise in the open air."

Ever yours.

LETTER XXXV.

Palermo, July 27th.

THE Sicilians are animated in conversation, and their action for the most part is so just and so expressive of their sentiments, that without hearing what is said, one may comprehend the subject of their discourse. We used to think the French and Neapolitans great adepts in this art; but they are much outdone by the Sicilians, both in the variety and justness of their gesticulation.

The origin of this custom they carry so far back as the time of the earliest tyrants of Syracuse, who, to prevent conspiracies, had forbid their subjects, under the most severe penalties, to be seen in parties talking together. This obliged them to invent

a me-

a method of communicating their sentiments by dumb show, which they pretend has been transmitted from generation to generation ever since.

I think it is not at all improbable that this custom too may have given the first idea of comedy; as we find, that some short time after, Epicarmus, a native of that city, was the author of this invention.

The Sicilians till lately retained a great many foolish and superstitious customs; but particularly in their marriage and funeral ceremonies: it would be tedious to give you an account of all these; some of them are still practised in the wild and mountainous parts of the island.—As soon as the marriage ceremony is performed, two of the attendants are ready to cram a spoonful of honey into the mouths of the bride and bridegroom; pronouncing it emblematical of their love and union, which they

hope

hope will ever continue as sweet to their souls, as that honey is to their palates.—They then begin to throw handfuls of wheat upon them, which is continued all the way to the house of the bridegroom. This is probably the remains of some ancient rite to Ceres, their favourite divinity, and they think it cannot fail of procuring them a numerous progeny:—however, the Sicilian women have no occasion for any charm to promote this, as, in general, they are abundantly prolific even without it. Fazzello gives an account of women having frequently upwards of forty children; and Carrera mentions one who had forty-seven.

The young couple are not allowed to taste of the marriage-feast; this they pretend is to teach them patience and temperance; but when dinner is finished, a great bone is presented to the bridegroom by the bride's father, or one of her nearest relations, who pronounces these words: *" Rodi tu quest'*
" osso,

" *offo*, &c. Pick you this bone, for you have
" now taken in hand to pick one, which you
" will find much harder and of more dif-
" ficult digeftion."—Perhaps this may have
given rife to the common faying, when
one has undertaken any thing arduous
or difficult, that " He has got a bone to
" pick."

The Sicilians, like moft other nations in
Europe, carefully avoid marrying in the
month of May, and look upon fuch marriages as extremely inaufpicious. This
piece of fuperftition is as old, perhaps older
than the time of the Romans, by whofe
authors it is frequently mentioned; and by
whom it has been tranfmitted to almoft
every nation in Europe. It is fomewhat
unaccountable, that fo ridiculous an idea,
which can have no foundation in nature,
fhould have ftood its ground for fo many
ages.—There are indeed other cuftoms ftill
more trivial, that are not lefs univerfal.—

That

That of making April fools on the firſt day of that month; the ceremony of the cake on Twelfth-night; and ſome others that will occur to you, of which, no more than this, I have ever been able to learn the origin.

The marriages of the Sicilian nobility are celebrated with great magnificence; and the number of elegant carriages produced on theſe occaſions is aſtoniſhing. I wanted to diſcover when this great luxury in carriages had taken its riſe; and have found an account of the marriage of the daughter of one of their viceroys to the duke of Bivona, in the year 1551. It is deſcribed by one Elenco, who was a ſpectator of the ceremony. He ſays the ladies as well as gentlemen were all mounted on fine horſes, ſumptuouſly capariſoned, and preceded by pages: that there were only three carriages in the city, which were uſed by invalids who were not able to ride on horſeback. Theſe
he

he calls *Carette,* which word now fignifies a little cart.

The Sicilian ladies marry very young, and frequently live to fee the fifth or fixth generation. You will expect, no doubt, that I fhould fay fomething of their beauty:—In general, they are fprightly and agreeable; and in moft parts of Italy they would be efteemed handfome.—A Neapolitan or a Roman would furely pronounce them fo.—But a Piedmontefe would declare them very ordinary;—fo indeed would moft Englifhmen.—Nothing fo vague as our ideas of female beauty: they change in every climate; and the criterion is no where to be found.—

" Afk where's the North?—at York, 'tis on
   the Tweed,
" In Scotland at the Orcades, and there,
" At Nova Zembla, or the Lord knows where."

No two nations,—perhaps no two men, have affixed precisely the same characteriftics; and every one exalts his idea of it, according to the beauty of the women he is accuftomed to fee; fo that even the fame perfon may fometimes appear beautiful, fometimes ugly, juft in proportion as we have feen others that are more or lefs fo.— I remember, after making the tour of Savoy and the Lower Valais, every woman we met in Switzerland appeared an angel. The fame thing happens in travelling through fome parts of Germany; and you will eafily recollect the furprifing difference betwixt a beauty at Milan and one at Turin, although thefe places lie adjacent to each other. It is a pity that the Juno of Zeuxis has been loft, if it were no more than to have fhewn us the notion the ancients had of a perfect beauty. Indeed, the Venus of Medicis has been confidered as a model of perfection,—but it is furely abfurd; for

who

who ever heard of a perfect beauty of five feet high!—the very idea is ridiculous; and whatever figure her goddeſship might make amongſt the ancient divinities, in the pantheon at Rome, I am afraid ſhe would cut but a ſorry one amongſt the modern ones, in that of London.—In ſhort, I believe we may ſafely conclude, that beauty is a relative quality, and the *To kalon* is no longer the ſame, no more in a phyſical than a moral ſenſe, in any two places on the globe.

The ladies here have remarkable fine hair, and they underſtand how to dreſs and adorn it to the greateſt advantage. It is now only uſed as an embelliſhment; but in former times we are told, that, like that of Sampſon, it was found to be the ſtrength and protection of their country.—There is a paradox for you, that all the wiſe men of the Eaſt could hardly ſolve.—Their hiſtorians relate, (in whoſe reign I believe is

rather

rather dubious) that this city had suffered a long siege from the Saracens, and was greatly reduced by famine; but, what distressed them still more, there were no materials to be found for making bowstrings, and they were on the point of surrendering.—In this dilemma, a patriotic dame stepped forth, and proposed to the women, that the whole of them should cut off their hair, and twist it into bowstrings: This was immediately complied with.—The heroism of the women, you know, must ever excite that of the men.—The besieged, animated by this gallant sacrifice of the fair, renewed their defence with such vigour, that the assailants were beat off; and a reinforcement soon after arriving, the city was saved.—The ladies still value themselves on this story, which you may believe has not been forgotten by their bards.—
" The hair of our ladies (says one of their
" quaint poets) is still employed in the
" same office; but now it discharges no
" other

" other shafts but those of Cupid ; and the
" only cords it forms are the cords of
" love."

The Sicilians are much fonder of study than their neighbours on the continent; and their education is much more attended to. We were a good deal surprised to find, that instead of that frivolity and nothingness, which so often constitute the conversation of the Italian nobility, here their delight was to talk on subjects of literature, of history, of politics, but chiefly of poetry; for the other branches of knowledge and science are only general: this is the only one that may be said to be universal. Every person in some period of his life, is sure to be inspired; and a lover is never believed so long as he can speak of his passion in prose; and, contrary to our way of reasoning, is only reckoned true in proportion as he is poetical. Thus, inspiration,

ration, you fee, has here become the teft of truth.

We were aftonifhed on our firft arrival at Palermo, to hear ourfelves addreffed in Englifh, by fome of the young nobility; but ftill more fo, to find them intimately acquainted with many of our celebrated poets and philofophers.—Milton, Shakefpeare, Dryden, Pope, Bacon, Bolingbroke we found in feveral libraries, not in the tranflation, but generally in the beft editions of the original.

Our language, indeed, has become fo much in vogue, that it is now looked upon as no immaterial part of a polite education: the viceroy, the Marquis Fogliano, a man of great merit and humanity, has made fome of our authors his favourite ftudy, and greatly encourages the progrefs it is making in his kingdom. Many of of the nobility speak it a little; and some of them even with ease and fluency, although they have never been out of their island. The Marquis Natali, the Counts Statela and Buschemi, the Duke of St. Micheli, &c.; in whose company we have enjoyed a great deal of pleasure, and whose knowledge and erudition is the least part of their praise. Adieu.

Yours, &c.

LETTER XXXVI.

Palermo, July 28th.

I HAD almoſt forgot to ſay any thing of the opera:—It would have been very ungrateful, for we have been much delighted with it. The firſt and ſecond man, are both admirable ſingers, and I make no doubt you will have them in London in a few years; neither of them are as yet known, and I dare ſay at preſent they might be engaged for a very moderate price; but in Italy they will ſoon be taught to eſtimate their value.—The name of the firſt is Pacherotti; he is very young, and an entire ſtranger in the muſical world; yet I am perſuaded, that after he has been heard on the different theatres in Italy, he will be eſteemed one of their capital performers. His excellence is the pathetic, at preſent

too

too much neglected on most theatres; and indeed, I think, he gives more expression to his *cantabile* airs, and makes his hearers feel more, because he feels more himself, than any that I have seen in Italy. He indeed addresses himself to the heart, while most of the modern performers sing only to the fancy.

The first woman is Gabrieli; who is certainly the greatest singer in the world: and those that sing on the same theatre with her must be capital, otherwise they never can be attended to. This indeed has been the fate of all the other performers, except Pacherotti; and he too gave himself up for lost, on hearing her first performance.—It happened to be an air of execution, exactly adapted to her voice, which she exerted in so astonishing a manner, that before it was half done, poor Pacherotti burst out a crying; and ran in behind the scenes; lamenting that he
had

had dared to appear on the fame ftage with fo wonderful a finger; where his fmall talents muft not only be loft, but where he muft ever be accufed of a prefumption, which he hoped was foreign to his character.

It was with fome difficulty they could prevail on him to appear again, but from an applaufe well merited, both from his talents and his modefty, he foon began to pluck up a little courage ; and in the finging of a tender air, addreffed to Gabrieli in the character of a lover, even fhe herfelf, as well as the audience, is faid to have been moved.

Indeed, in thefe very pathetic pieces, I am furprifed that the power of the mufic does not fometimes altogether overcome the delufion of character; for when you are mafter of the language, and allow the united power of the poetry, the action, and
the

the mufic, to have its full force on the mind, the effect is wonderfully great.—However I have never heard that this happened completely but once; and it was no lefs a finger than Farinelli that produced it.—He appeared in the character of a young captive hero, and in a tender air was foliciting mercy for his miftrefs and himfelf of a ftern and cruel tyrant who had made them his prifoners. The perfon that acted the tyrant was fo perfectly overcome by the melting ftrains of Farinelli, that inftead of refufing his requeft as he ought to have done, he entirely forgot his character, burft into tears, and caught him in his arms.

The performance of Gabrieli is fo generally known and admired, that it is needlefs to fay any thing to you on that fubject. Her wonderful execution and volubility of voice have long been the admiration of Italy, and has even obliged them to invent a new term to exprefs it; and would

would she exert herself as much to please as to astonish, she might almost perform the wonders that have been ascribed to Orpheus and Timotheus; but it happens, luckily perhaps for the repose of mankind, that her caprice is, if possible, even greater than her talents, and has made her still more contemptible than these have made her celebrated. By this means, her character has often proved a sufficient antidote, both to the charms of her voice and those of her person, which are indeed almost equally powerful; but if these had been united to the qualities of a modest and an amiable mind, she must have made dreadful havoc in the world. However, with all her faults, she is certainly the most dangerous syren of modern times, and has made more conquests, I suppose, than any one woman breathing.

It is but justice to add, that contrary to the generality of her profession, she is by no means

means selfish or mercenary; but on the contrary, has given many singular proofs of generosity and disinterestedness. She is very rich; from the bounty, as is supposed, of the last emperor, who was fond of having her at Vienna; but she was at last banished that city, as she has likewise been most of those in Italy, from the broils and squabbles that her intriguing spirit, perhaps still more than her beauty, had excited. There are a great many anecdotes concerning her, that would not make an unentertaining volume; and, I am told, either are, or will soon be published.

Although she is considerably upwards of thirty, on the stage she scarcely appears to be eighteen; and this art of appearing young, is none of the most contemptible that she possesses.—When she is in good humour, and really chuses to exert herself, there is nothing in music that I have ever heard,

heard, to be compared to her performance; for she sings to the heart, as well as the fancy, when she pleases; and she then commands every passion with unbounded sway. But she is seldom capable of exercising these wonderful powers; and her caprice and her talents exerting themselves by turns, have given her, all her life, the singular fate of becoming alternately an object of admiration and of contempt.

Her powers in acting and reciting, are scarcely inferior to those of her singing; sometimes, a few words in the recitative, with a simple accompaniment only, produces an effect, that I have never been sensible of from any other performer; and inclines me to believe what Rousseau advances on this branch of music, which with us is so much despised. She owes much of her merit to the instructions she received from Meteftasio, particularly in acting and reciting;

ing; and he allows that she does more justice to his operas than any other actress that ever attempted them.

Her caprice is so fixed and so stubborn, that neither interest, nor flattery, nor threats, nor punishments, have the least power over it; and it appears, that treating her with respect or contempt, have an equal tendency to increase it.

It is seldom that she condescends to exert these wonderful talents; but most particularly if she imagines that such an exertion is expected. And instead of singing her airs as other actresses do, for the most part she only hums them over, *a mezza voce*. And no art whatever is capable of making her sing, when she does not chuse it.

The most successful expedient has ever been found, to prevail on her favourite lover, for she always has one, to place himself in the centre of the pit, or the front box; and if they are on good terms, which is seldom the case, she will address her tender airs to him, and exert herself to the utmost.—Her present enamorato promised to give us this specimen of his power over her; he took his place accordingly; but Gabrieli, probably suspecting the connivance, would take no notice of him; so that even this expedient does not always succeed.

The viceroy, who is fond of music, has tried every method with her to no purpose. Some time ago he gave a great dinner to the principal nobility of Palermo, and sent an invitation to Gabrieli to be of the party. Every other person arrived at the hour of invitation. The viceroy ordered dinner to be kept back, and sent to let her know that the company waited her. The messenger found her reading in bed;—she said she was sorry for having made the company wait,

wait, and begged he would make her apology, but that really she had entirely forgot her engagement.

The viceroy would have forgiven this piece of insolence, but, when the company came to the opera, Gabrieli repeated her part with the most perfect negligence and indifference, and sung all her airs in what they call *sotto voce*, that is, so low, that they can scarcely be heard. The viceroy was offended; but as he is a good-tempered man, he was loth to make use of authority; but at last, by a perseverance in this insolent stubbornness, she obliged him to threaten her with punishment in case she any longer refused to sing.

On this she grew more obstinate than ever, declaring that force and authority should never succeed with her; that he might make her cry, but that he never could make her sing. The viceroy then sent

sent her to prison, where she remained twelve days. During which time, she gave magnificent entertainments every day; paid the debts of all the poor prisoners, and distributed large sums in charity. The viceroy was obliged to give up struggling with her, and she was at last set at liberty amidst the acclamations of the poor.— Luckily for us, she is at present in good humour, and sometimes exerts herself to the utmost of her power.

She says she has several times been on terms with the managers of our opera, but thinks she shall never be able to pluck up resolution enough to go to England. What do you think is her reason?——It is by no means a bad one. She says she cannot command her caprice; but, for the most part, that it commands her; and that there she could have no opportunity of indulging it:—For, says she, were I to take it into my head not to sing, I am told the

people

people there would certainly mob me, and perhaps break my bones;—now I like to sleep in a sound skin, although it should even be in a prison.—She alleges too, that it is not always caprice that prevents her from singing; but that it often depends upon physical causes; and this indeed I can readily believe: for that wonderful flexibility of voice that runs with such rapidity and neatness through the most minute divisions, and produces almost instantaneously so great a variety of modulation, must surely depend on the very nicest tone of the fibres. And if these are in the smallest degree relaxed, or their elasticity diminished; how is it possible that their contractions and expansions can so readily obey the will, as to produce these effects?—The opening of the glottis which forms the voice is extremely small, and in every variety of tone, its diameter must suffer a sensible change; for the same diameter must ever produce the same tone:—So wonderfully

minute

minute are its contractions and dilatations, that Dr. Keil, I think, computes, that in some voices, its opening, not more than the tenth of an inch, is divided into upwards of 1200 parts, the different sound of every one of which is perceptible to an exact ear. Now, what a nice tension of fibres must this require!—I should imagine every the most minute change in the air, must cause a sensible difference, and that in our foggy climate the fibres would be in danger of losing this wonderful sensibility; or at least, that they would very often be put out of tune. It is not the same case with an ordinary voice; where the variety of divisions run through, and the volubility with which they are executed, bear no proportion to those of a Gabrieli.

One of the ballets of our opera, is a representation of Vauxhall gardens, and this is the third time I have seen Vauxhall brought upon the Italian theatre; at Turin, at at Naples, and here. The gardens are well reprefented, and the idea muft have been given by fome perfon that had been on the fpot. A variety of good Englifh figures are brought in: fome with large frizzled wigs fticking half a yard out behind their necks; fome with little cut fcratches, that look extremely ridiculous. Some come in cracking their whips, with buckfkin breeches and jockey caps. Some are armed with great oaken fticks; their hair tied up in enormous clubs, and ftocks that fwell their necks to double the natural fize. But what affords the principal part of the entertainment is, three quakers who are duped by three ladies of the town, in concert with three jack-tars, their lovers.—Thefe characters, as you may believe, are much exaggerated, though, upon the whole, they are fupported with humour, and have afforded us a good deal of laughing; however we were hurt to fee the refpectable character of quakers turned into such ridicule; and as the people here were altogether unacquainted with it, we have been at some pains to explain to them the simplicity and purity of their manners, and the incorruptible integrity of their principles.

Although the Sicilians in general are a good sort of people, and seem to be endowed with a large share of philanthropy and urbanity; yet it must be owned they have no great affection for their neighbours on the continent; and indeed the dislike is altogether reciprocal.—It is somewhat singular; I am afraid not much for the honour of human nature; that through all Europe, the two neighbouring nations have a perpetual jarring with each other.—I could heartily wish that we had been an exception from this rule; but am sorry to see, from our news-papers, which are sent to the

the nobility of this city, that at prefent, we are rather the moft diftinguifhed for it; at leaft our animofities, if there really are any, make by much the greateft noife of all.—We have often been afked by foreigners, what was the ground of the mighty quarrel, that fuch torrents of the moft illiberal abufe have been poured out by a people fo celebrated for liberality of fentiment; and it is with difficulty we can perfuade them, that although from the papers, this fometimes appears to be the voice of the nation, yet in fact, it is only confined to a fet of the moft worthlefs and defpicable incendiaries; like him who fet the houfe in a flame, on purpofe to pilfer during the conflagration.—But the abufe that is levelled at the king, furprifes them more than all the reft; and you cannot conceive their amazement and indignation when we affured them, that notwithftanding all this, he was the moft virtuous and benevolent prince on earth.— Then, exclaimed a Sicilian nobleman, you muſt certainly be the moſt damnable people on the globe.—I was a good deal ſtruck with the ſuddenneſs of the charge; and it was not without many explanations of the liberty of our conſtitution, and particularly that of the preſs, that I could prevail with him to retract his ſentiments; and think more favourably of us.—Still he inſiſted, that ſo egregious an abuſe of this liberty, was only a farther proof of his poſition; and that there muſt be ſomething eſſentially wrong, in a nation that could allow of ſuch abuſe levelled at the moſt ſacred of all characters: the higheſt virtue united to the higheſt ſtation. We aſſured him, that what he heard, was only the voice of the moſt abandoned and profligate wretches in the nation; who, taking advantage of the great freedom of the preſs, had often made theſe news-papers the

vehicles

vehicles of the moſt deteſtable ſedition. That both the king and queen were beloved by all their ſubjects, at leaſt by all thoſe of worth;—that they never were ſpoken of but as the moſt perfect model of conjugal union and happineſs, as well as of every ſocial endowment; and that they could have no enemies, but the enemies of virtue.

However, after all, we could but patch up a peace with him. He could not comprehend (he ſaid) how the voice of a few incendiaries ſhould be louder than the general voice of the nation.—We told him, that people who were pleaſed commonly held their tongue; and that ſedition and libel ever made a greater noiſe than panegyric; juſt as the fire-bell is rung louder, and is more liſtened to than the bell for rejoicing.

Adieu.

Adieu. Our pilot ſays the wind is not fair, ſo that poſſibly we may ſtill ſtay a day or two longer.

        Ever yours.

LETTER XXXVII.

Palermo, July 29th.

WERE I to enter upon the natural hiftory of this ifland, it would lead me into a vaft field of fpeculation, for which I have neither time nor abilities: However, a variety of objects ftruck us as we travelled along, that it may not be amifs to give you fome little account of.— There are a variety of mineral waters, almoft through the whole of Sicily. Many of thefe are boiling hot; others ftill more fingular, are of a degree of cold fuperior to that of ice, and yet never freeze.

In feveral places, they have fountains that throw up a kind of oil on their furface, which is of great ufe to the peafants, who burn it in their lamps, and ufe it to many other

other purpoſes; but there is ſtill a more remarkable one near Nicoſia which is called *Il fonte Canalotto*. It is covered with a thick ſcum of a kind of pitch, which amongſt the country people is eſteemed a ſovereign remedy in rheumatic, and many other complaints.

The water of a ſmall lake near Naſo is celebrated for dying black every thing that is put into it; and this it is ſaid to perform without the mixture of any other ingredient, although the water itſelf is remarkably pure and tranſparent.

They have a variety of ſulphureous baths, like thoſe near Naples, where the patient is thrown into a profuſe ſweat, only from the heat of the vapour. The moſt celebrated are thoſe of Sciaccia, and on the mountain of St. Cologero; not in the neighbourhood of Ætna, as I expected, but

but at a great diftance from that mountain. But indeed I am much inclined to believe, that not only mount Ætna, but the greateft part of Sicily, and almoft the whole of the circumjacent iflands, have been originally formed by fubterraneous fire; but I fhall have an opportunity of fpeaking more largely on this fubject, when I give you an account of the country round Naples.

I have obferved lava, pumice, and tufa in many parts of Sicily; at a great diftance from Ætna; and there are a variety both of mountains and valleys that ftill emit a hot vapour, and produce fprings of boiling water.

About a mile and a half to the weft of this city, at a fmall beach where we often go a fwimming, there are many fprings of warm water that rife even within the fea, at the depth of five or fix feet. We were at firft a good deal furprifed to find ourselves almost instantaneously both in the hot and cold bath; for at one stroke we commonly passed through the hot water, which only extends for a few feet around the spring. It gave us a momentary glow, and produced a very odd, uncouth sensation, by no means an agreeable one. I mentioned this singularity to several gentlemen here, who tell me they have observed the same thing.

Not a great way from this is a celebrated fountain, called *Il Mar Dolce*, where there are some remains of an ancient naumachia; and in the mountain above it they shew you a cavern, where a gigantic skeleton is said to have been found: however, it fell to dust when they attempted to remove it.—Fazzello says, its teeth were the only part that resisted the impression of the air; that he procured two of them, and that they weighed near two ounces.—There are many such stories to be met with in the Sicilian legends, as it seems to be an universal belief, that this island was once inhabited by giants; but although we have made diligent inquiry, we have never yet been able to procure a sight of any of these gigantic bones which are said to be still preserved in many parts of the island. Had there been any foundation for this, I think it is probable, they must have found their way into some of the museums; but this is not the case; nor indeed have we met with any person of sense and credibility that could say they had seen any of them. We had been assured at Naples, that an entire skeleton, upwards of ten feet high, was preserved in the museum of Palermo; but there is no such thing there, nor I believe any where else in the island. This museum is well furnished both with antiques and articles of natural history, but is not superior to what we have seen in many other places.

The number of souls in Palermo are computed at about 150,000. Those of the whole island, by the last numeration, amounted to 1,123,163; of which number there are about 50,000 that belong to the different monasteries and religious orders. The number of houses are computed at 268,120, which makes betwixt five and six to a house.

The great standing commodity of Sicily, which has ever constituted the riches of the island, was their crops of wheat; but they cultivate many other branches of commerce, though none that could bear any proportion to this, were it under a free government, and exportation allowed. Their method of preserving their grain will appear somewhat singular to our farmers: instead of exposing it, as we do, to the open air, they are at the greatest pains to exclude it entirely from it.—In many places, where the soil is dry, particularly near

near Agrigentum, they have dug large pits or caverns in the rock. Thefe open by a fmall hole at top, and fwell to a great width below; here they pour down their grain, after it has been made exceedingly dry; and ramming it hard, they cover up the hole, to protect it from rain; and they affure us it will preferve in this manner for many years.

The Soda is a plant that is much cultivated, and turns out to confiderable account. This is the vegetable, that by the action of fire, is afterwards converted into mirrors and chryftals. Great quantities of it are fent every year to fupply the glafshoufes at Venice.—They have likewife a confiderable trade in liquorice, rice, figs, raifins, and currants, the beft of which grow amongft the extinguifhed volcanoes of the Lipari Iflands. Their honey is, I think, the higheft flavoured I have ever feen; in fome parts of the ifland even

fuperior

superior to that of Minorca: this is owing, no doubt, to the quantity of aromatic plants, with which this beautiful country is every where overspread. This honey is gathered three months in the year; July, August, and October. It is found by the peasants in the hollows of trees and rocks; and is esteemed of a superior quality to that produced under the tyranny of man.— The country of the Lesser Hybla is still, as formerly, the part of the island that is most celebrated for honey. The Count Statela made us a present of some of it, gathered on his brother the Prince of Spaccaforno's estate, which lies near the ruins of that city.

Sugar is now no article of the Sicilian commerce, though a small quantity of it is still manufactured for home-consumption; but the plantations of the sugar-cane, I am told, thrive well in several parts of the island.

The

The juice of liquorice is prepared both here and in Calabria, and is sent to the northern countries of Europe, where it is used for colds.—The juice is squeezed out of the roots; after which it is boiled to a consistency, and formed into cakes, which are packed up with bay-leaves in the same order that we receive them.

In some of the northern parts of the island, I am told, they find the shell-fish that produces a kind of flax, of which gloves and stockings are made; but these two are found in greater quantities in Calabria.

Their plantations of oranges, lemons, bergamots, almonds, &c. produce no inconsiderable branch of commerce. The pistachio-nut too is much cultivated in many parts of the island, and with great success. These trees, like many others, are
male

male and female; the male is called *Scor-nobecco*, and is always barren; but unlefs a quantity of thefe are mixed in every plantation, the piftachio-tree never bears a nut.—But of all the variety that is cultivated in Sicily, the manna-tree is efteemed the moft profitable; it refembles the afh, and is I believe of that fpecies. About the beginning of Auguft, during the feafon of the greateft heat, they make an incifion in the bark, near to the root of the tree; a thick whitifh liquor is immediately difcharged from the wound, which foon hardens in the fun, when it is carefully taken off and gathered into boxes. They renew thefe incifions every day during the feafon, obferving, however, only to wound one fide of the tree; the other fide they referve for the fummer following.

The cantharides-fly is a Sicilian commodity; it is found on feveral trees of Ætna, whofe

whofe juice is fuppofed to have a corrofive or abfterfive quality, particularly the pine and the fig-tree; and I am told the cantharides of Mount Ætna are reckoned preferable to thofe of Spain.

The marbles of Sicily would afford a great fource of opulence, were there any encouragement to work the quarries: of thefe they have an infinite variety, and of the fineft forts. I have feen fome of them little inferior to the giall and verd antiqua, that is now fo precious. The beautiful yellow columns you muft have obferved in the royal chapel of Cafferto are of the firft kind. They have likewife fome that very much refemble lapis lazuli and porphyry.

At Centorbi they find a kind of foft ftone that diffolves in water, and is ufed in wafhing inftead of foap, from which property
it

it is called *Pietra Saponaro*. They likewise find here, as well as in Calabria, the celebrated stone, which, upon being watered and exposed to a pretty violent degree of heat, produces a plentiful crop of mushrooms:—But it would be endless to give you an account of all the various commodities and curious productions of this island; Ætna alone affords a greater number than many of the most extensive kingdoms, and is no less an epitome of the whole earth in its soil and climate, than in the variety of its productions.—Besides the corn, the wine, the oil, the silk, the spice, and delicious fruits of its lower region; the beautiful forests, the flocks, the game, the tar, the cork, the honey, of its second; the snow and ice of its third; it affords from its caverns a variety of mineral and other productions; cinnabar, mercury, sulphur, allum, nitre, and vitriol; so that this wonderful mountain at the same time

produces

produces every neceſſary and every luxury of life.

Its firſt region covers their tables with all the delicacies that the earth produces; its ſecond ſupplies them with game, cheeſe, butter, honey; and not only furniſhes wood of every kind for building their ſhips and houſes, but likewiſe an inexhauſtible ſtore of excellent fewel; and as the third region, with its ice and ſnow, keeps them freſh and cool during the heat of ſummer, ſo this contributes equally to keep them warm and comfortable during the cold of winter.

Thus, you ſee, the variety of climates is not confined to Ætna itſelf; but, in obedience to the voice of man, deſcends from that mountain; and mingling the violence of their extremes, diffuſes the moſt benign influences all over the iſland, tempering
each

each other to moderation, and softening the rigours of every season.

We are not then to be surprised at the obstinate attachment of the people to this mountain, and that all his terrors have not been able to drive them away from him: for although he sometimes chastises; yet, like an indulgent parent, he mixes such blessings along with his chastisements, that their affections can never be estranged; for at the same time that he threatens with a rod of iron, he pours down upon them all the blessings of the age of gold.

Adieu. We are now going to pay our respects to the viceroy, and make our farewel visits.—This ceremony never fails to throw a damp on my spirits; but I have seldom found it so strong as at present, there being little or no probability that we shall ever see again a number of worthy people

people we are juft now going to take leave of, or that we fhall ever have it in our power to make any return for the many civilities we have received from them.

Farewell. The wind we are told is fair, and I fhall probably be the bearer of this to the continent, from whence you may foon expect to hear from, &c.

LETTER XXXVIII.

Naples, August 1st.

AFTER two days delightful sailing, we have again arrived in this city; where, to our infinite joy, we have found all the worthy friends we had left behind us. This indeed was necessary, to wipe out the impressions which the leaving of Sicily had occasioned. We shall still remain here, at least for three months, till the season of the *Mal Aria* is entirely over. You know the danger of travelling through the Campania during that season; which although it is looked upon by many of our learned doctors as a vulgar error, yet we certainly shall not submit ourselves to the experiment.

We propose to pass the winter at Rome, where we shall probably find occupation enough for four or five months.—From thence by Loretto, Bologna, &c. to Venice; the old beaten track.—We shall then leave the parched fields of Italy, for the delightful cool mountains of Switzerland; —where liberty and simplicity, long since banished from polished nations, still flourish in their original purity; where the temperature and moderation of the climate, and that of the inhabitants, are mutually emblematical of each other.—For whilst other nations are scorched by the heat of the sun, and the still more scorching heats of tyranny and superstition; here the genial breezes for ever fan the air, and heighten that alacrity and joy which liberty and innocence alone can inspire;— here the genial flow of the soul has never yet been check'd by the idle and useless refinements of art; but opens and expands itself to all the calls of affection and benevolence.

volence.—But I muſt ſtop. You know my old attachment to that primitive country.— It never fails to run away with me. We propoſe then, to make this the ſcene of our ſummer pleaſures; and by that time, I can foreſee, we ſhall be heartily tired of Art, and ſhall begin again to languiſh after Nature. It is ſhe alone that can give any real or laſting pleaſure, and in all our purſuits of happineſs, if ſhe is not our guide, we never can attain our end.

Adieu, my dear friend. You have been our faithful companion during this Tour, and have not contributed a little to its pleaſure. If it has afforded equal entertainment to you, we ſhall beg of you ſtill to accompany us through the reſt of our travels. A man muſt have a miſerable imagination indeed, that can be in ſolitude, whilſt he has ſuch friends to converſe with; the conſideration of it ſoon removes the mountains and ſeas that ſeparate us, and

SICILY AND MALTA. 355

and produces thefe fympathetic feelings, which are the only equivalent for the real abfence of a friend; for I never fit down to write, but I fee you placed on the oppofite fide of the table, and fuppofe that we are juft talking over the tranfactions of the day. And without your prefence to animate me, how is it poffible that I could have had patience to write thefe enormous epiftles?—Adieu. We are foon going to make fome excurfions through the kingdom of Naples: and if they produce any thing worthy of your obfervation, we muft beg that you will ftill fubmit to be one of the party.

I ever am,

Moft fincerely and affectionately, yours,

PAT. BRYDONE.

FINIS.

www.ingramcontent.com/pod-product-compliance
Lightning Source LLC
Chambersburg PA
CBHW020315240426
43673CB00039B/809